MW00336985

© Louise Bouchard 2013

Edmond Theriault   **Brian J. Theriault**

Leaving Tracks:
A Maine Tradition

By Brian J. Theriault and Edmond Theriault
Master Snowshoe Makers

First published May 2014 (MMXIV)

© Copyright Theriault's Snowshoes, Brian J. Theriault

Hard cover: ISBN 9780991006908
Soft cover: ISBN 9780991006991
Ebook: ISBN 978099106915

All Rights Reserved

No portion of this publication may be produced, stored in any electronic system, or transmitted in any form or by any means, electronic, mechanical, photocopy, recording, or otherwise, without written permission from the author, Brian J. Theriault.

Brian J. Theriault
P.O. Box 242
Fort Kent Mills, ME 04744
U.S.A

theriaultsnowshoes@gmail.com
ilovesnowshoes.com
796.92
Publisher: Brian J. Theriault
Editors: Edmond Theriault, Louise Latvis, Joseph W. Davis, Mike Lareaux, Brian J. Theriault
Technical Assistance: Garry Bouchard, John Bartlett, Benjamin Latvis, Brian J. Theriault
Design: Brian J. Theriault, Louise Latvis
Diagram of ash tree: Andy Latvis
Cover Picture: Louise Bouchard
Family Picture: Jerry Jalbert
Black and white picture: Cedric Chatterley
Photographs: Brian J. Theriault, Joan Theriault, Louise Latvis, Louise Bouchard, Ty Coates, Joseph W. Davis

Aroostook County, Maine, USA
Printed in the United States of America

Contents

Diagrams/Charts/Pictures

Preface

I believe that, in the beginning, people came to northern Maine to get away from conditions that existed where they lived. They came in the summer when the weather was pleasant and the food was abundant. There were very few people, since many died when the cold weather and winter snow set in. To survive, transportation was needed to get to where the caribou and deer spent the winter. In deep snow, it was indeed difficult. The survivors found that, if they stepped on large spruce branches tied to their feet, they did not sink as much in the snow. That's where the snowshoe was born. No doubt, they attached branches to their feet and walked on the snow. The only materials these first snowshoe makers could use were wood and rawhide. This is still the best and traditional method. Every snowshoe maker since that day has made his own improvements until it developed into an art form. Even today, if you want to go anywhere in deep snow, you need a good pair of traditional snowshoes made of wood and rawhide.

Edmond Theriault
2011

Native People made the first snowshoes and generously taught the new comers to North America how to make them. Hunters, fishermen, loggers, and trappers required snowshoes to travel through the harsh winters of Maine, Canada, and any other places with snow. My father, Edmond Theriault, who is 91 years old at this writing, started making snowshoes out of need. Unable to afford snowshoes for his eleven children, wife, or himself, my father sought out information available in the community and learned some of the skills needed to make snowshoes. He also began repairing snowshoes and gained a wealth of knowledge by studying the construction and materials used on these local examples. I was with my father from the first skin and the first tree. I will tell you, we wish we had the book and DVD when we started. It took a lot of time and hard work to learn this knowledge; it is information that can save so many hours and strenuous labor. You do not have to be rich, but you do need time and persistence to make your own pair of traditional snowshoes.

Brian J. Theriault

Introduction

     This book is written by Brian and Edmond Theriault to help preserve the art of traditional snowshoe making. Many hours have been spent learning and developing the process to make the best snowshoes for snow traveling and exercising. The design and workmanship is the bonus that creates a work of art.

     My father remembers that in the 1930's, the roads around Fort Kent, Maine were not open for certain parts of the winter. Every family had snowshoes, especially the hunters and trappers. The Roy family was making snowshoes with ash trees and rawhide to sell for $2.00 a pair.

     My father and I started making snowshoes over forty years ago when one of the last old snowshoe makers in Fort Kent, Willie Roy, was retiring. He was very helpful in showing us the tools he was using and what to look out for when choosing a tree and preparing rawhide. We are grateful for Willie's help in preserving this art form. We have been at it ever since.

     Making snowshoes can be looked at as more of a hobby, but underneath it all, it is a great chance to save a small part of the history of this area. We have made many changes and used different tools to save time and improve quality. Being from a family of hunters and trappers gave us an extra reason to travel to where the animals lived during our harsh winters.

"The world changes by taking small steps; leaving tracks so they can be followed."
By Brian J. Theriault

Snowshoes
Where the past meets the future.
Where the old and young get together.
Where old and new stories are made.
    When one put traditional snowshoes on.
    When out on a white deep snowy blanket.
      It just feels cool.
      It just feels fun.
      It just feels right.
Where the past meets the future.
Where the old and young get together.
Where old and new stories are made.
    When one puts traditional snowshoes on.
    When out on a white deep snowy blanket.
      One thing is for sure.
      One thing is for heath.
      One thing is just for you.
The place where dreams are made.
The place the ground and air meet.
The place where you meet the snow.
    When one puts traditional snowshoes on.
    When out on a white deep snowy blanket.
      Let the snow come down.
      Let it snow.
      Let the snow be deep.
The place where dreams are made.

By Brian J. Theriault

Part 1 - How It Started

Chapter 1 - My Early Life

Black Ash Tree, Eagle Lake, Maine

As far back as I can remember, I have been around my dad, learning all kinds of things that helped me to better understand my environment. My father has been a great part of my dream. I think that a lot of what I learned was because of how my father taught me. We worked together, learning and exchanging ideas, creating Theriault's Snowshoes. I was around my father so much that I learned how to think and make projects with a creative mind. I learned a hands-on do-something-about-it attitude. I developed a work ethic that helped me to see the importance of continually moving forward with my ideas and the process of snowshoe making.

Photograph by Cedric Chatterley

I grew up in a large, loving family. My parents, who have reached their sixy-first anniversary this year, have eleven children. They include, from the oldest to youngest: Alvin, Wanda, Brian (myself), Galen, Anne, Louise, Marian, Lila, Aileen, Laurie, and Edmond Jr. (Eddie). The house was always a busy place. There were quarrels at times, but there was always enough love to bring understanding. Each one of us would do whatever we could to help each other when in need. Mostly, we learned to rely on ourselves and to work hard to achieve our goals.

Photograph by Jalbert

Besides my father, my paternal grandfather, Joseph Theriault, was an important figure in my life. My grandfather was a great outdoorsman and knew how to survive. He was a storyteller and a singer. He recorded hundreds of folk songs before he died. He was a great man that struggled to not only help his own large family, but also many families in the community survive difficult times. Edmond talks about his father: "My father did not start making snowshoes because he could make more money trapping. Snowshoes cost about two dollars, and he could get a lot more money with fox furs. Farmers would grow small plots of ground with buckwheat, oats, and potatoes. Farmers grew peas too, but those were only good for pea soup. Mice would even eat the potatoes. With so many mice in the fields, there were many foxes. It did not take long for fox families to multiply. The large number of foxes made it worth the extra work, trapping, to help the family survive."

"TRAPPER JOE"
Joseph T. s/o Arsene T.
& Olive T.

10

Money was a factor when my father started to make snowshoes. All eleven children wanted snowshoes, but there was no money to purchase them. My father has a "can do it, just do it," mindset, and he applies it to everything he does. It might be hard, but it is okay to have to put in some work. He was raised with the belief that it was good to work hard and to be proud of what you do. His first snowshoes were made with much experimentation. He never seemed to be satisfied with what he had done, and his mind continued to think through better ways to make snowshoes. From faster and easier ways to handle the wood for weaving the webbing, my father and I developed original ways to make Theriault's Snowshoes.

Growing up in the small town of Fort Kent in northern Maine, where the white flakes fall eight months out of the year, snow has always been a big part of my life. I spent most of my time outdoors. I liked clean air and blankets of snow on the ground, which Maine has in abundance. I called snow "white gold." We always had so much of it that I thought everyone must know what snow was. It was part of my life for the majority of the year.

I participated in many outdoor activities because that was where I was the most comfortable. I spent most of my time outdoors, hunting, fishing, and trapping. I was never too lucky at hunting. Trapping was a learning experience, though. I learned to have patience when positioning traps to have the best results. Skinning the animals gave me skills in working with skins. Also important was the right location.

Much of the time, I could be found standing in brooks, streams, and rivers, learning the best ways to catch fish. I dug worms in the garden or went night crawling for bait. I fished in the many Maine waterways, including the Fish River, St. John River, and Eagle Lake. I also fly fished and ice fished, trolling with home-made chrome spoons and rudders, always catching my share within the fishing limit and throwing a lot of fish back in the water. I often brought fish home to give to my mom. Most of all, hunting, fishing, and trapping gave me a better understanding of animals and the environment.

I also enjoyed working with wood when I was younger. As a young adolescent, I showed an interest and natural ability in working with wood. I helped to build things and used tools for carving. I would work on wood projects, helping to make or fix things to gain a better understanding of wood. I worked on ash basket making, taking all day to pound a log with my brothers. Woodworking helped me improve my snowshoe making skills. My father took me on as an apprentice and taught me how to make and repair snowshoes. He would look at what had to be done, look around at what he had, and develop a solution to achieve his overall plan. My

father and I work so well together! It is not only on snowshoes, but other things also. Even today, I still am learning from my father and working with him.

My interest in wood continued with college courses. I graduated at the University of Maine at Fort Kent with an Associate of Arts Degree in Forestry. My training at Eastern Maine Vocational Technical College included the course: Pulp and Paper Industry. I took courses at Washington County Technical College in Woodland and Harvesting Practices. At Northern Maine Technical College, my diploma was in Carpentry.

Note:

Chapter 2 - History of Snowshoe Making

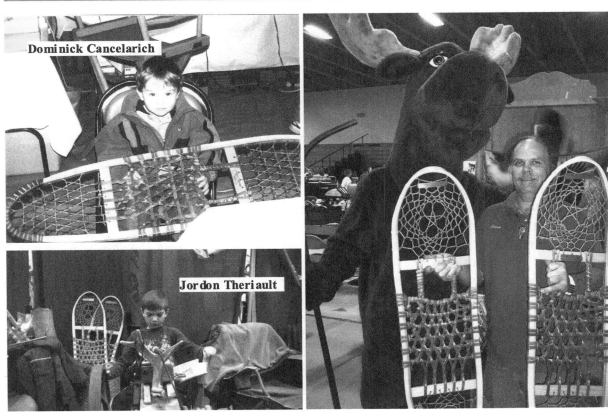

Dominick Cancelarich

Jordon Theriault

In Alaska and Canada, it is well known that snowshoes were used a lot. There are many pictures of natives and other people, in old photographs, with snowshoes or with people using snowshoes. It was expensive and hard with older cameras. I think this shows how people depended on snowshoes and used them all the time. It was such a big a part of life; it was a treasured necessity. If you asked most people back then what was the most important tool of transportation, it would be snowshoes, even over the use of canoes. It takes a lot more time to make a canoe than a pair of snowshoes.

Knowledge about snowshoeing is a way to connect with the past. Maine has an important history with snowshoes. Norway, Maine was known as the snowshoe capital of the world in the 1800's and 1900's. Maine ancestors were proud of their snowshoes, and it was quite something if you had a pair. It was like owning a horse in the west. All that was needed was a pair of snowshoes and leather bindings to live. Now, I would like Theriault's Snowshoes in Maine to become the new snowshoe capital of the world. I am keeping the art of traditional snowshoe making alive, not only with my DVD and book, but by going around giving demonstrations and talking about snowshoes. It is my lifelong dream and commitment, sharing my knowledge of this usable transportation method and revealing a great work of art.

Snowshoe Construction

The best way to understand the traditional techniques in snowshoe construction is to study the shape, how the wood was cut and bent, how they were woven, and what was used to weave it. Branches could be used to make snowshoes, but usually this creation did not hold together very long. Makers would sometimes use smaller trees and split them into four strips for two pairs of snowshoes. Bone tools were used. Copper and even rocks were also used. The crooked knife and an ax were often used for snowshoe making and for any applications involving wood.

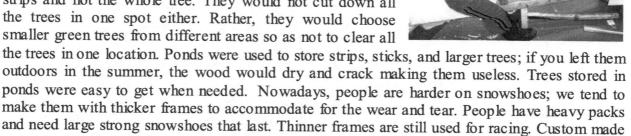

A wooden shaving/whittling horse and a hand draw shaver were used to take shavings of wood from a stick to shape it. The wood frames of snowshoes back then were thinner, and it was easier to bend. They could be made light, but still durable. Snowshoes strips, a lot of time, were made right in the woods. The maker would only bring back the strips and not the whole tree. They would not cut down all the trees in one spot either. Rather, they would choose smaller green trees from different areas so as not to clear all the trees in one location. Ponds were used to store strips, sticks, and larger trees; if you left them outdoors in the summer, the wood would dry and crack making them useless. Trees stored in ponds were easy to get when needed. Nowadays, people are harder on snowshoes; we tend to make them with thicker frames to accommodate for the wear and tear. People have heavy packs and need large strong snowshoes that last. Thinner frames are still used for racing. Custom made snowshoes are made for the needs of the owner.

Bones and rocks were also used to make snowshoes. They helped cut rawhide and control fire to make steam to bend snowshoes. A hot steaming temperature was used on the sticks for the bending of the tree. This would limit the splintering of the wood. Steaming was a difficult process that required a great deal of time, control, and concentration. Sharp rocks were used for sanding the wood. Very few other tools were needed for the actual making of snowshoes. Placing skins in brooks or other bodies of water was useful to remove the hair. In the fall, rocks were put onto the skin to help hold the skin in place. They had to check them often so that the skin would not rot away. Rawhide was cut with a sharp rock to form straight two-foot strips. Fine weaving was developed into patterns that were used on the snowshoes. The actual weaving was made with a bone net-type needle. Many knots were used to hold the rawhide together because, back then, it was hard to cut long continuous pieces of rawhide.

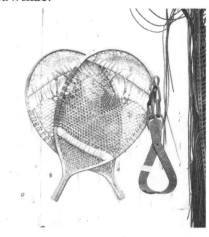

There are many shapes of snowshoes and many different designs.

Courtesy of Roger B. Greene Collection.

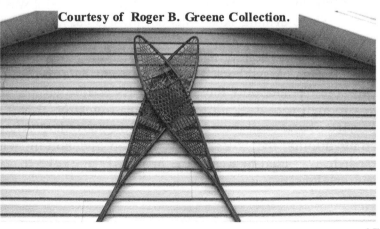

Molds were sometimes just a board or boards put together to hold the frame's shape as one snowshoe was made at a time. The thicker planks were used to make one pair at a time. The upward bending of the front top ends was a lot of work, and was relatively rare in traditional snowshoes. They did not have a rack like we use today that helps keep the front end shaped when storing).

The skin scraping was done with an old file that was ground with a grinding wheel to form a rounded end. The file was curved at the tip, about one inch wide. A piece of wood was used for the handle. After the skin was fleshed, this tool was used to scrape the hair off. It took a lot of time to cover very much area on the hide, and it was hard to do smoothly.

Since drilling holes was not always easy, some makers used the one-hole pattern at the ends. This was done with the older snowshoes. The rawhide lacing was pushed through the hole to the outside, then yarn, hair, or something durable was put to hold the outside loop. The rawhide was passed back through the same hole to continue working on the weaving. With the two-hole method, only fine rawhide was used to go into the holes. The finer rawhide was harder to size and more difficult to cut into narrow strips, but it was needed for the small holes on the front (top) and back (bottom) parts of the snowshoe. After the first circle of rawhide was woven going through the holes around the top and bottom with the thinner rawhide, a little wider rawhide was used to weave the inside of the circle. It was easier to cut wider rawhide without continually sizing it.

Fine-rawhide weaving was sometimes used in the center to show the skill of the craftsman. The fine weaving was not done often, probably because of the difficulty of cutting the narrow rawhide with the limited tools and the time it took to complete. These snowshoes needed to be fixed often. The problem was, one weak spot and the rawhide would start to break. This fine rawhide tended to look good but broke at pressure points. There were also a lot of knots in the weaving. The lacing would break easily if used with hard soles; hard soles would wear

the rawhide more quickly. Soft sole moccasins were often used when walking on the snowshoe middles with fine rawhide centers. The skill of fine weaving without a paper drawing was a badge of honor among snowshoe makers. The thick cow rawhide used today can withstand the harder rubber soles of modern boots.

Weaving patterns were very important for the functional use of snowshoes. The back-and-forth weaves worked, but they did not look good and moved easily with the body's stepping motion. It was a problem when there was a lot of weave movement, loosening the pattern. The modified hole sizes in the weaving limited the bounce. It took a while for the three-way weaving pattern to be developed as the best way to weave the snowshoes.

Later, in about the 1950's, metal and plastic snowshoes came into the picture. These mass-produced snowshoes did not take the natural world or the benefits of environmental knowledge into account. People who bought them might as well be putting metal trays on their feet! The wood and webbing of wooden snowshoes allow for the give and take of man and snow. It is all-natural, supporting an environmentally friendly earth.

People back then seemed to be smaller. The lower weight is indicated because of the size of the snowshoes we have seen. We have had to craft a big bear paw for heavy guys weighing over 350 pounds. Without this, they would not go snowshoeing. We always have to change with

the times and adapt to the styles that people like and need. How they look, how they work, and how they are made are all important. People will seek a traditional snowshoe maker out because they know what they want, and it is not necessarily available in the limited market of metal, egg-shaped, machine-made models. There is a big difference when they learn about Theriault's snowshoes, which are more individualized. Each pair of snowshoes tells a story that has a meaning to the individual person.

Snowshoe Makers

Snowshoes were traded and used all the time. In fact, people did not go anywhere in the winter without snowshoes. They were convenient and imperative to have when traveling. They were also something of which to be proud of. A lot of time was put into making snowshoes back then. Winters were long and you had to do something. Snowshoe makers would get most of their rawhide in the fall and use it throughout the extended winter. The

skills were passed on, and there were a lot of snowshoe makers. Still, it was usually done as an individual task. People would develop an expertise that could be continually perfected. Snowshoe makers had status in their area and were well respected. They were well known to many people in a large region.

Some snowshoe makers brought the snowshoe mold with them in the woods to make the frames near the tree. The sticks would be bent over some hot coals or maybe over steam from birch bark containers. This is why you might see some old snowshoes with burn marks on the tip of the wood. There were few books, if any back then, describing how to make snowshoes. It was a skill passed down by family members. The reason for wider snowshoes might have been that they were easier to make because they required less sharp wood-bending at the top. There was less chance of the wood splitting. It also made sense that the larger surface area would keep a person higher on the snow. When long narrow snowshoes came into the picture, it improved performance by making it a more comfortable walk.

Within many tribes, women would weave after the men got the tree and bent the sticks into frames. Usually, within a tribe, one person did not make the snowshoes by themselves. Snowshoe makers might differentiate tribes with pom-pom colors or designs on snowshoes. Snowshoe making is one of the known traditions that have been passed on among all northern

tribes. I know of one tribe in Canada where most of the people in the tribe, through teamwork, worked on snowshoes to help the tribe survive. They would work hard!

Many snowshoe makers might get very little money. Some people made a living selling snowshoes for snowshoe makers. The makers had to do a good job or they would not be able to give them away! If one of the maker left or died, only the ones who were shown what to do would know how to continue. If the knowledge was not shared and no one knew the craft, that maker's skills would stop there.

There are still a few snowshoe makers alive now, and they are mostly older. My father and I have gained a lot of knowledge from past makers by looking at their actual snowshoes, but we like weaving our own snowshoe patterns. In the next few years, I may be the only one with over 50 years of snowshoes making skills at my age because I started young. I love making snowshoes and teaching others how to make them.

Personal History of Snowshoe Making
My dad talks about how he started:

Willie Roy was an older snowshoe maker, in his eighties, who had made snowshoes his whole life. He was finishing his snowshoe projects to retire. I went to see him one or two times. The first time, he did not show me much. He talked about different things that had happened in his life. When I asked him how much he was getting for snowshoes during the depression, he answered that they were selling them, snowshoes and harnesses, for two dollars a pair. During the winter, the whole family made a hundred pairs of snowshoes.

The second visit, he showed me how he steamed the wood to make it bend better. He showed me how he cleaned his skins, taking the hair off. He showed me how to cut the rawhide. He also weaved the center of one snowshoe showing me the knots at the sides.

This knowledge gave me a starting point. I made a couple of round snowshoes to better understand his process. Once I had a grasp of how he did it, I developed the methods further. Using my own awareness of the environment, I could see that boiling wood might weaken it. Removing the hair could be done in less time with greater ease by using lime and ash solutions. The soft rawhide was easier to cut, but it was harder to control the width of the strip when cutting. I figured that with partially softened rawhide, the pressure needed to cut rawhide could be lessened by using the weight of a heavy wheel.

The knots he was making for the center of the snowshoe were not very complicated. Once I looked at the finished center, I could see how the curve of the knots seemed to make the center like a bowl that would hold snow, rather than pushing it off or allowing it through. The old timers would say, "Ce ne sasse pas bien le neige." (It does not sift the snow very well.) I turned the knots upward, making the snowshoes more effective.

Many of the master snowshoe makers have passed away, taking their knowledge with them. Much information about the art has been lost. My father and I are some of the very few who are left to carry on with this remarkable tradition. I remember when dad and I first started making snowshoes. It was such a big job because we had to make everything, mostly by trial

and error. For example, the tree was split and shaped into individual sticks by removing the strips from the tree. The sticks were difficult to cut straight and the knots in the wood had to be avoided. We use a combination of old and new methods to make snowshoes more efficiently.

Bending the wood was an arduous job, especially when we started. We had to take a three-foot plank, 2 inches thick by 12 inches wide, to manipulate the tail of the frame onto the mold. Using the holes drilled into the plank and two three-foot pipes, the tails of the snowshoes were bent together to make a matching set. What a grueling job! A lot of force, almost two peoples' worth, was needed to hold the tail together as the shape of the snowshoe was determined with the support of the mold, then clamped to hold it in place. One tricky job was

using the edge of broken glass, off a single pane of a window, to do the sanding on the wooden frame pieces. All of the sanding was done by hand. It used to take a lot of time to make a pair of snowshoes, 30 or more hours.

Another difficult process was cutting the small rawhide. We used a stand up blade attached to a table when we started. We pulled a small piece of similar thickness cow skin by hand as we cut the rawhide. A lot of force was needed and the cuts were often uneven. We would drill three different size holes into a piece of wood to pass all the small one six inch rawhide through. First, it needed to be passed through the biggest hole, then the medium hole. Lastly, the strip had to be passed through the right size hole, the smallest hole. All this work was required before weaving it onto the snowshoes. It was tedious work. It had to be good rawhide to make it worth our time.

The big rawhide was cut with the same standing blade stuck on the table. It was more difficult because the hide was thicker and more difficult to pass through the blade. Uneven thicknesses would show more on the center of the snowshoe and be more difficult to control when weaving straight places. It became quite easy when we finally started using a heavy wheel to pull the rawhide through the cutting blade. That was a skill all by itself to learn!

Every task was a big job! We had to figure out how it could be done easier and faster. My father and I had to do everything on our own. With the many small tasks in the process, the time factor limited the completion of work. My father and I talked about what we were doing and how

we could do it better. When we went on trips to events, we would talk about information and ideas. I would say: "How about this?" and he would say: "How about that?" We would bounce different ideas off each other. Then we would go back to the workshop to try it. We were looking for ways to save time and make the snowshoes better.

We repaired a lot of snowshoes made by others. We gained ideas from them and learned how to make ours better. We did not want ours returned, so we always kept the highest quality in mind. Old snowshoes are hardly used today because their width is uncomfortable to walk with and the rawhide weakens with time and wear. Soft soled boots or moccasins should be used with older snowshoes. Looking at snowshoes of the past helped us discover a world of ingenuity. Today, we do not like to fix snowshoes made by others, because we would rather utilize our own quality work that lasts. People do not want to pay adequately for fixing old snowshoes, and we do not have the time for additional tasks.

Even today, improved methods can be developed. If someone wants to make a lot of snowshoes, methods could be developed to save time and keep the quality. I think we have lost so much that it will be hard to understand what went into them in the past. It is quite something now because there is so much interest in our snowshoes. We always have a following of people that come to see us at events. Some say they got a pair before, and they tell how much they like them. Some people have multiple pairs of our Theriault's Snowshoes.

I was glad to learn one weekend, when I was working with my father, that Glenn Labbe, a friend of mine, was interested in snowshoe making. He really liked learning how to weave his own pair of snowshoes. My father looked like he was having a good time helping to teach Glenn. At 91 years of age, my father continues to be curious about the process of different crafts, which he sometimes uses to further his own skills. It is great to watch and work with a master snowshoe maker. I am proud of my father and glad I am his son.

A lot of people are just starting to realize what has been lost and want to help. My father and I have worked hard to keep the quality and workmanship of our snowshoes. Although snowshoes have taken a back seat to automation at times, people continue to use the historically tried-and-true traditional snowshoes. People do not always recognize how important good time-tested and time-honored snowshoes are. They have a place today in their usefulness and a place in our history. There is a big difference owning a great pair of snowshoes that are crafted with skill and quality materials: wood and rawhide, which we call Theriault's Snowshoes, "A Maine Tradition".

Jordan Labbe

Hudson Labbe

Jordan Theriault

Madison Theriault

Benjamin Latvis

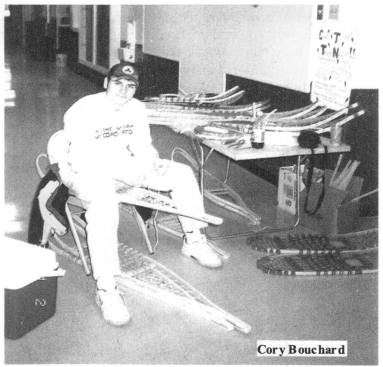

Cory Bouchard

Notes:

Chapter 3 – Snowshoe Planning

A. Front (top) end of snowshoes
B. Notched front crosspiece

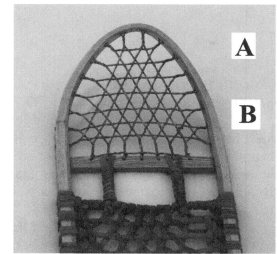

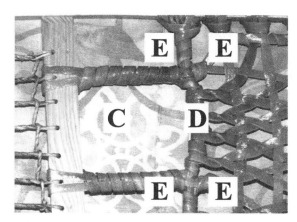

C. Square toe hole, big because of today's big boots
D. Main strand with wrapping on top of it
E. Binding slot on each side

F. Heavier rawhide weaving around frame back

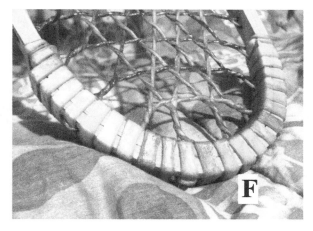

G. Drill holes top and bottom

H. Back crosspiece, further back for today's bigger boot, to walk or run easier.

I. Lighter rawhide on the front end, through the v-notch between the outside frame side holes decreases the chance of it breaking against the crust of the snow. The bigger holes in the weaving are to let the snow out and still give support. This causes the snow to slide off and through the snowshoe.

J. The center rawhide knots on the side grips on the snow when moving. The pre-stretching of the rawhide allows your foot to bounce.

Tools

Keep safety in mind during each step. Dull tools can be more dangerous than sharp tools. My dad and I have tried to keep safety in mind when making tools and using them. This project has many tools that were developed to make the tasks easier and to save time and money. Often, we had to use materials around us to invent better tools! Some of the tools you might buy. They do not have to be expensive ones; keep in mind the use and practicality of the tool.

The shaving horse is a tool I started using for demonstrations. The person sits at one end, and by pressing on the foot pedal, holds the usually green wood. This allows the use of the two-handed draw shaver. This works really well to shape a snowshoe stick. Leather can also be placed between the clamps and the wood to protect the strip. It is great to use your foot to hold your work, making it fast and easy to work with two hands.

Hand Tools

Hand Scraper

Rubber Gloves

Sled to Haul Trees

Two-Handed Big Flesher

Plastic Apron

Florescent Orange Ribbon

Increment Borer

Magnifying Glass

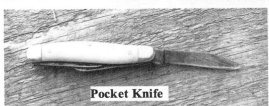

Pocket Knife

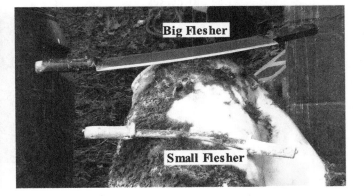

Big Flesher

Small Flesher

Peavey

Log Sawhorses

Moose-Shed Crooked Knife

Wood Draw Shaver

Hammer

Handmade Filed-Ends Wood Chisel

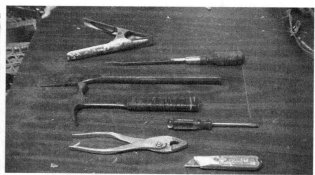

Block-and-Tackle

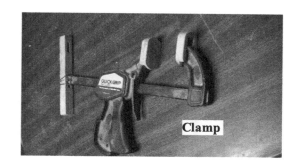

Clamp

Leather Hole Punch

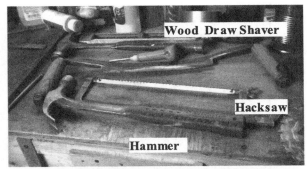

Wood Draw Shaver

Hacksaw

Hammer

Table vice

Utility Knife

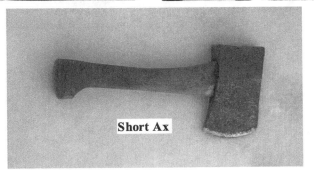

Short Ax

Electric Tools

Electric Hand Grinder

10 Inch Table Saw

8 Inch Skill Saw

Electric Hand Drill

Drill Press

Homemade Tools

Jig for making crosspiece angles

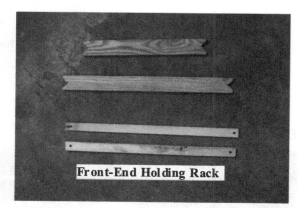

Front-End Holding Rack

Tail end jig for long tail
with a 2-ton jack

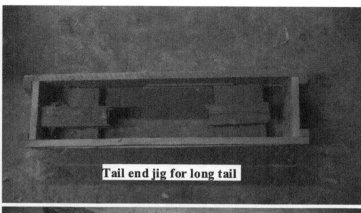

Tail end jig for long tail

Back end bender (modified bear paws)

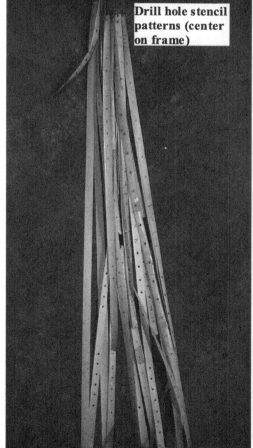

Drill hole stencil
patterns (center
on frame)

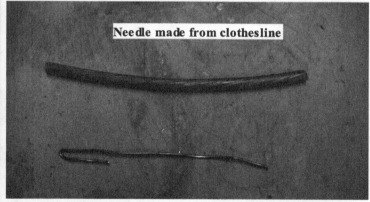

Needle made from clothesline

Wide rawhide cutting tool

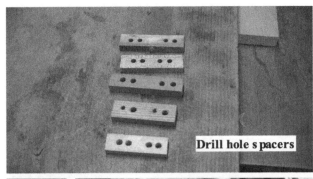

Drill hole spacers

Hop On Pop snowshoe chair

Table vice w/wooden jaw

Center rawhide stretcher block with a two ton jack

Fleshing beam and plastic barrel's

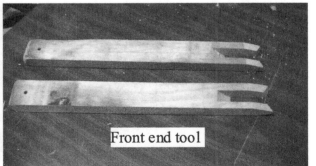

Front end tool

Other Equipment

Notes:

Chapter 4 - Snowshoe Types

Snowshoe Frames

We have gone through a process of discovery as we developed different types of frames. Some of the snowshoes have become out of style and bulky. Looking at old snowshoes, we could see that width, length, and weaving were the most important components for snowshoe makers. My dad saw one thing wrong, which was that snowshoes were too wide. People had only thought of purpose, walking on snow, not comfort. The wide ones worked and people were willing to buy or trade for them. They did not know the reasons why things were done that way. Wide snowshoes made for a very uncomfortable waddle. Not only are you walking with spread legs, but also you are using a lot of uncomfortable energy and muscle force to work through the deep snow. A narrower snowshoe makes for a more comfortable stride. Styles have changed as the needs of modern day tasks vary. Keeping with the times and with top of the line traditional snowshoes is my goal. My intention is to develop a work of art that is usable, reliable, and comfortable.

A. Large Cross Country
B. Large Modified Green Mountain Bear Paw
C. Ojibwa (top picture, prior page)

A   **B**

The two types of snowshoes that we have found that are the best and in the greatest demand are the modified green mountain (bear paw) snowshoes and cross-country snowshoes. These two types of snowshoes are the only snowshoes we make in two sizes with different custom widths. They are sought the most and work the best. The modified bear paw snowshoes work well in wooded areas. The cross county snowshoes are my favorites because I can walk between two trees easily fitting in narrow places. For breaking trail, the large cross country are the best for coverage and the 6-inch raised front tips help in very deep snow. The narrow cross-county shoes glide through the soft snow. There is some demand for the Ojibwa snowshoes, which use shorter pieces for the frame and have more of a native flare. The crosspieces control the width of the snowshoes with the tail as a rudder to keep snowshoes pointing forward.

We do not make too many children's snowshoes because kids grow up so fast, and they do not use them much before they are outgrown. They take just as much time to make as an adult pair. For children, it is best to wear a larger pair and grow into them. The larger sizes are light and narrow, which can be used by younger people. A smaller size could be made by just downsizing the mold and other parts to make it fit. We do make small snowshoes for running, with no crosspieces, no tail, and all big rawhide weaving.

Our family has made some small pairs of snowshoes that look great on walls, and later even mini ones that can be worn on a necklace or as earrings. They take time to make with little profit. That is why there are very few people that make them anymore. The demand is limited and they are not as functional as traditional snowshoes.

Molds

Most people make their own molds because it is sometimes hard to copy other molds. Maybe, they want to do their own thing. Mostly, the knowledge and the molds were passed down; there was no schooling for this knowledge. Makers used their own markings, like painting red and black snowshoe tails, which I have seen in Canada. It seems people like to put in their own touches. Even with my father and I, we do things a bit different. We can tell that our snowshoes are different. When I look at molds and old snowshoes, I learn so many things. It is like looking at a timeline picture book. For me, it says a lot, and helps me learn the in's and out's of my craft.

Molds that are made of wood work the best. They can be made out of recycled wood or planks. Low-cost wood for the mold is good enough because new wood will not necessarily mean a better finished frame. It might just be more expensive. A good mold makes it easier and faster to make frames. I am making some molds now out of cedar wood, which will be lighter to handle when hanging it up higher, next to the ceiling, to dry faster. Still, a minimum of ten or eleven days is needed and frames are left on the molds to keep their shape until the frames or the molds are needed. Keep the frames in a dark place if you are going to store them a few months or more because they will lose their color in light. Some makers used flat sticks to shape the mold, which I think is much harder to use than the regular mold. Making one frame at a time, the finished frames might not be similar to each other when joining the pair to make a set.

Molds are used to hold the frames and are made in many different ways. Dad and I use the back-to-back mold, which gives better control for the drying process. We make a pair at a time, keeping the strips evenly placed side-by-side, back-to-back. Back-to-back molds give the end product more uniformity, and this achieves the best results. These molds are fast and easy to work with. If the snowshoe frames are not even, a bit of wood can be added to the

side or the wood can be sanded to equalize the two pieces. Clamp the bumps to straighten out the frames to pull in the bumps. The clamp can be put on a wooden mold at the spot needed to be straightened out. If there is no place for a clamp on the mold, a one inch hole can be drilled on the mold to take off bumps by clamping the frame and mold together.

Making molds is pretty easy. (See mold patterns at end of this chapter.) Just take a piece of paper and try it on a small scale. If it looks good, make it on a big scale by folding a thicker paper in half, cutting it once, and opening it up so both sides are the same. Put it on thin

hardboard and make more molds if needed. Mold designs can easily be made by taking a thick piece of cardboard and folding it in half. The pattern can be formed, cut, and used to make the wooden mold. The mold can even be made from two boards. The important thing is that the molds are even on both sides to make great looking frames. We are now making the mold with a spruce 2-inch by 4-inch stud going the length of the mold so the tail for cross-country snowshoes can be straightened. The mold keeps the frames in place, and they easily slide off when dried. Some molds use square crosspieces or braces to hold the frames apart to dry after taking them off the regular mold.

The tail end of the cross-country needs a jig with a 2-ton jack to help push it on the mold faster. This is hard to do by hand. The jack rig helps to easily and quickly clamp the ends together and a plywood c-clamp helps hold it together as you release the jack. This happens really fast, and you need to be careful that you do not mar the frames. Be really careful when bending the front end to keep the wood from splitting. To start, make sure to clamp that first bend slowly. Then bend the other side. Other wooden tools are used to help bend the fronts and backs of frames.

Snowshoes tell a story about the people who made and used them. We figure where some snowshoes come from by observing the shape and the type of wood used. Snowshoe styles tell about the conditions of the snow they were used in. One board mold, which I found in a Fort Kent garage, was given to me for a few bucks. It was just a board. The maker would have made one snowshoe frame at a time. They would have waited for the time it took to dry before they

could make the second frame for the pair. This might have been okay for them. They might have just wanted to make a few snowshoes or had two separate molds to make a set at the same time. They might have been using the materials they had at the time and thought it was an easier way, or maybe, they had never seen a back-to-back mold.

I have seen wooden pegs on molds instead of spikes, like we use today, to hold the stick in the mold. I have made an all-metal mold for long cross-country shoes with the toe bent up just like it should be. This works really well and the wood can be clamped to the metal frame anywhere there is a bump. It is not perfect, but if you mark them and use the two frames on the same side of the mold, it tends to make a more perfect frame. Other people make all kinds of different molds. I come across many stories about snowshoe frames or someone who knew about different snowshoe makers.

It looks like there are fewer and fewer molds out there. I have been collecting molds, which someday soon will be used for my museum. People with old wooden molds often just burned them or threw them away. Many times, people who had old molds looked at them as scraps of wood. They had no use for them, and they took up space. They did not care. Snowshoe history was lost as they were destroyed. Molds are important because they can tell a lot about the maker, and there is meaning in the snowshoes' shape. Even if you do not know the makers' name, the information is invaluable. Skills were passed on or forgotten. It was a different world back then. These molds are part of the craft. That is why I collect everything I find that relates to snowshoes. I am making a data bank that could be used to keep all this information. If knowledge is lost, we lose.

All our mold holes are pre-drilled and bolted together with quarter inch bolts.

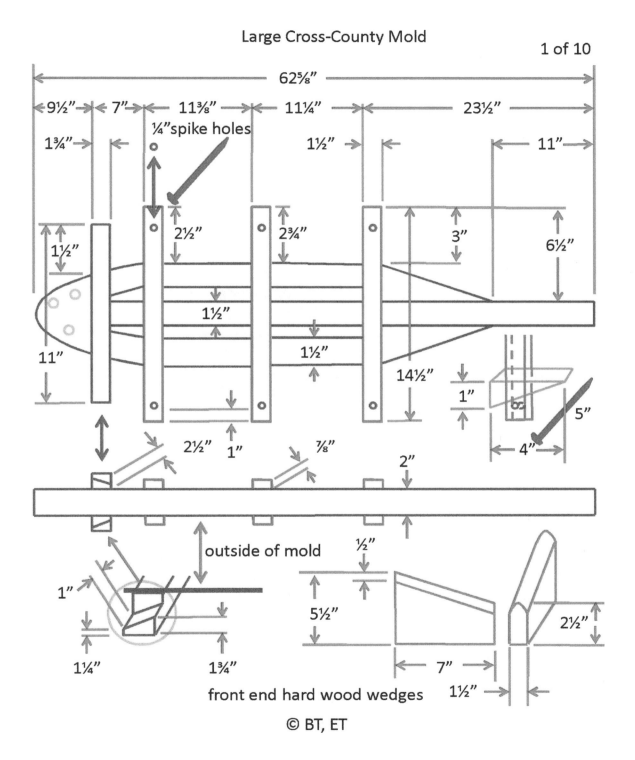

front end hard wood wedges

© BT, ET

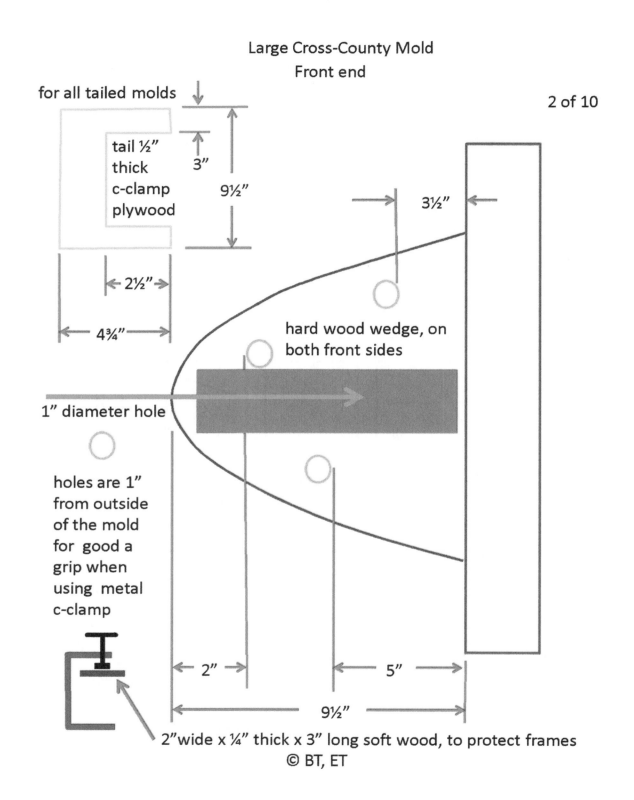

Large Cross-County Mold
Front end

for all tailed molds

tail ½" thick c-clamp plywood

3"

9½"

3½"

2½"

4¾"

hard wood wedge, on both front sides

1" diameter hole

holes are 1" from outside of the mold for good a grip when using metal c-clamp

2"

5"

9½"

2"wide x ¼" thick x 3" long soft wood, to protect frames
© BT, ET

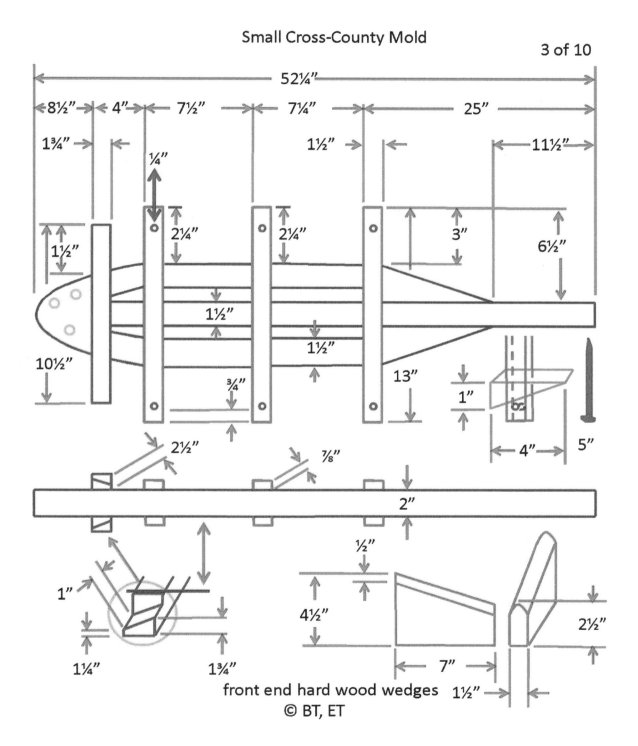

front end hard wood wedges
© BT, ET

Small Cross -County Mold

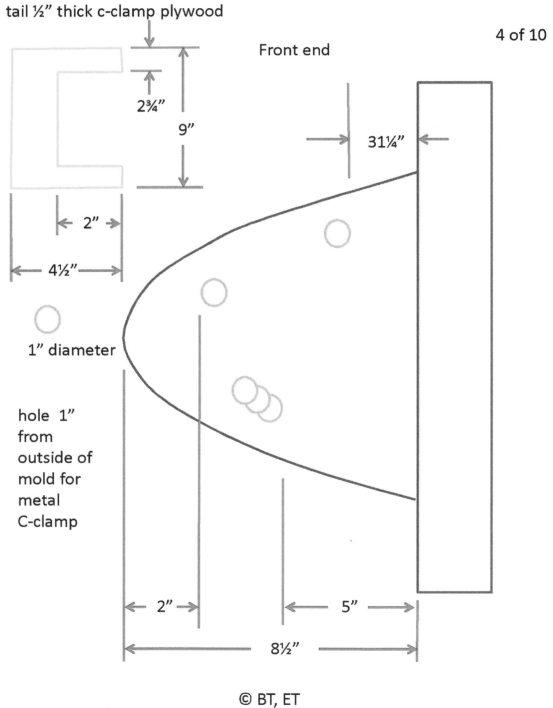

tail ½" thick c-clamp plywood

Front end

2¾"

9"

31¼"

2"

4½"

1" diameter

hole 1"
from
outside of
mold for
metal
C-clamp

2"

5"

8½"

© BT, ET

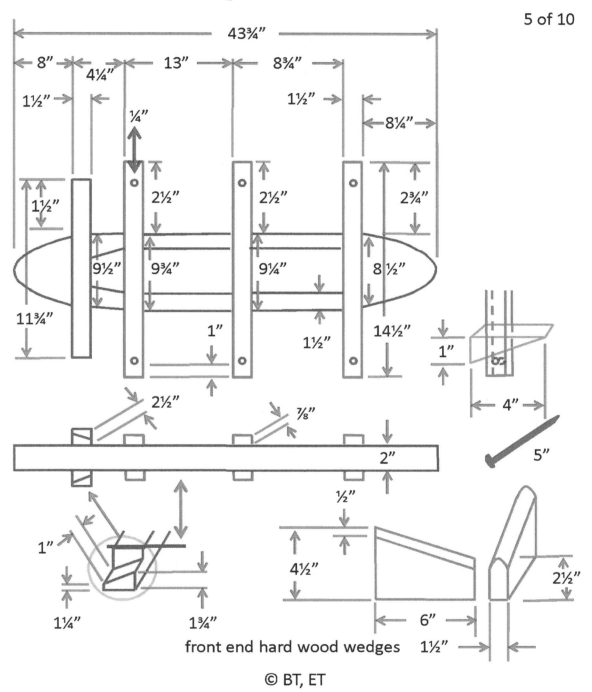

front end hard wood wedges

© BT, ET

Large Green Mountain Mold

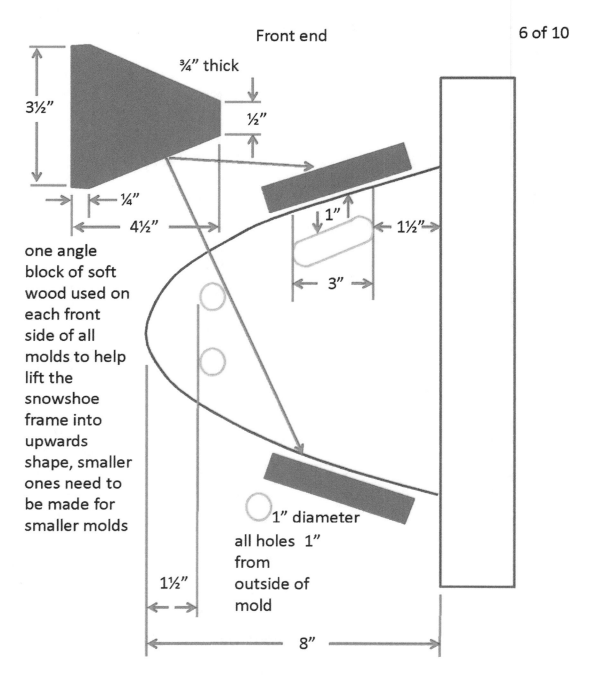

¾" thick

3½"

½"

¼"

4½"

1"

1½"

3"

one angle block of soft wood used on each front side of all molds to help lift the snowshoe frame into upwards shape, smaller ones need to be made for smaller molds

1" diameter all holes 1" from outside of mold

1½"

8"

© BT, ET

Large Green Mountain Mold

Back end

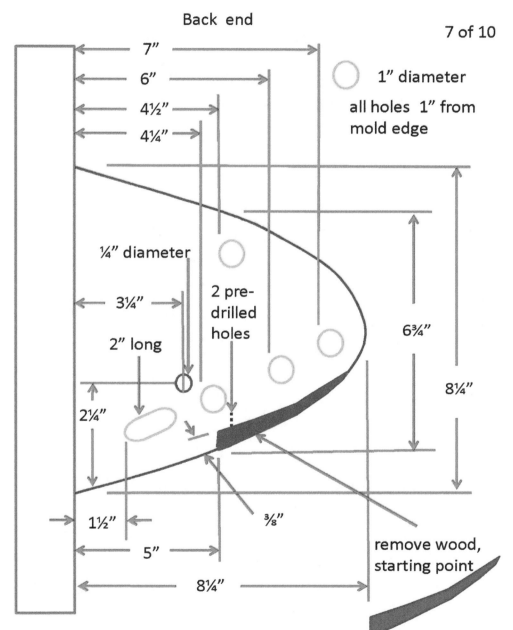

7"

6"

4½"

4¼"

1" diameter

all holes 1" from mold edge

¼" diameter

3¼"

2 pre-drilled holes

2" long

6¾"

8¼"

2¼"

1½"

⅜"

5"

remove wood, starting point

8¼"

see SGM back end mold for metal plate, may have to make it with more of a space for screws, to fit frames

© BT, ET

Small Green Mountain Mold

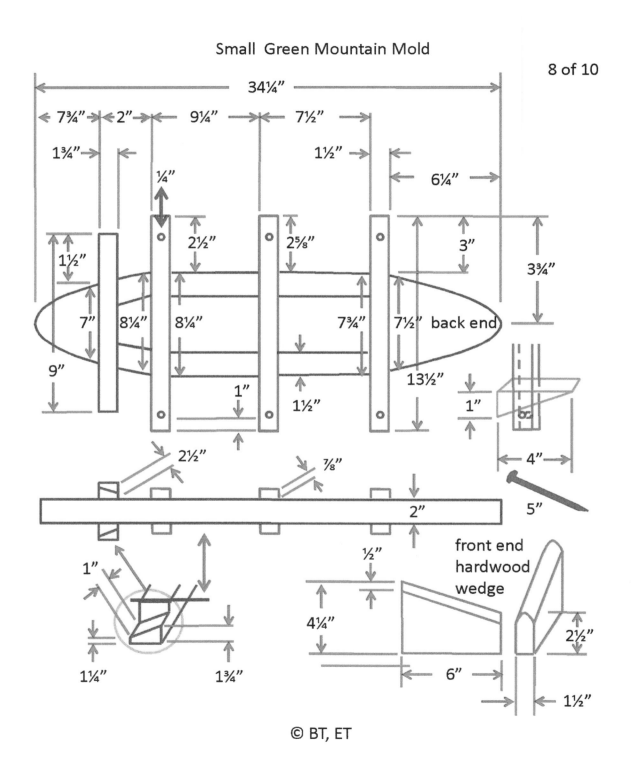

© BT, ET

50

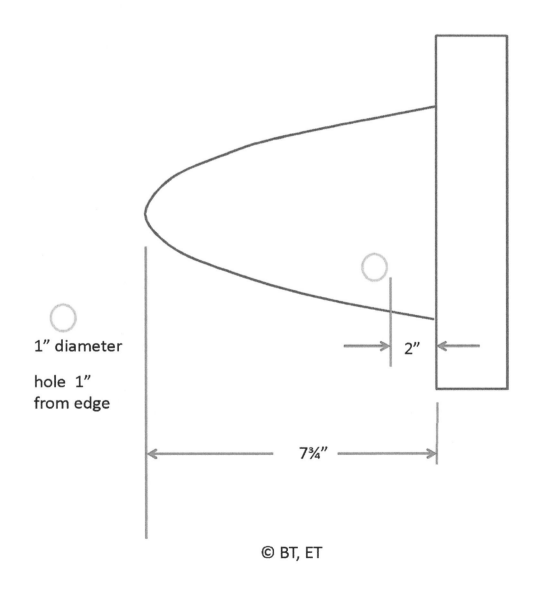

1" diameter

hole 1"
from edge

7¾"

2"

© BT, ET

Small Green Mountain Mold

Back end

1" diameter   holes 1" from outside of mold

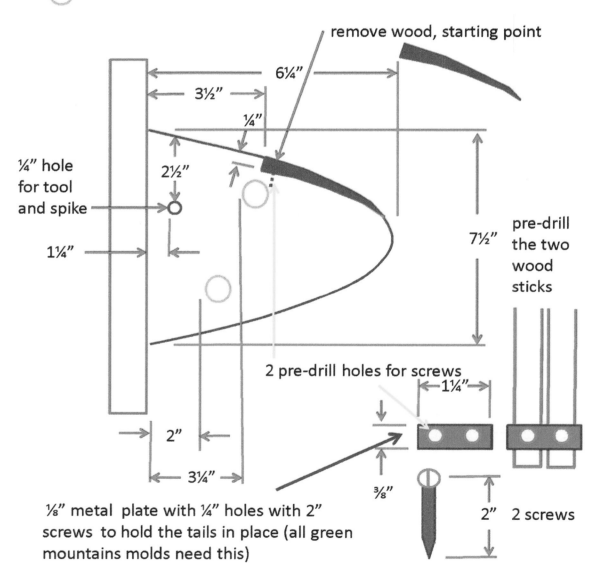

remove wood, starting point

6¼"

3½"

¼"

2½"

¼" hole
for tool
and spike

1¼"

7½"

pre-drill
the two
wood
sticks

2 pre-drill holes for screws

1¼"

2"

3¼"

⅜"

2" 2 screws

⅛" metal plate with ¼" holes with 2"
screws to hold the tails in place (all green
mountains molds need this)

© BT, ET

Notes:

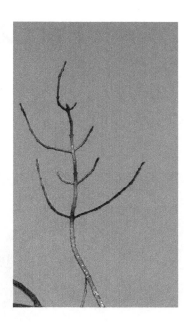

Part 2 - Making the Snowshoes

Chapter 5 - Wood

Please keep in mind as you continue reading that it is important to use good wood and materials to make an exceptional handmade pair of snowshoes. Everything is done for a reason; do not get discouraged. Like anything, it takes practice to master any skill. Above all, follow the illustrations exactly as shown in the book. Take your time. The process will become easier and faster, especially after you have made your hundredth pair! Always keep safety in mind when doing each task. You never know when the unexpected will happen. Take your time and work the best you can.

Selecting the Tree

Most of the trees we use are called brown ash (Fraxinus nigra - Latin name). At times, we call them black ash, basket ash, or swamp ash. The branches are opposite, rather than alternate. They have pinnate compound leaves, meaning the leaves are opposite each other on a branch. They have five to eleven leaflets. Young trees have smooth bark.

Brown ash trees are common in northern Maine. You need to follow the same process for both black ash trees and white ash trees. Black ash and white ash trees are

worked green, clear of damage and knots, if you can get them. Since we make snowshoes that require strips of different lengths, we can use the wood below the knots. The outside of snowshoes is the outside of the tree. Keep that in mind when working the tree. Snowshoes strips are taken right off the tree with a skill saw and squared off and shaped on the table saw. This technique is used the most because it is fast and easy. Black or white-ash trees are the perfect wood for snowshoes.

We choose trees that are fairly straight and have a healthy look. We can see this by looking at the top and by looking at the bark grain going up and down the tree. The bark should not be twisted, and you want fewer knots. Warped grains will not work well. Wood with larger pores, which cannot be seen with your bare eyes, has more give and bends better. A good tree, that is growing well, can be bent green without steam. This retains the strength of the strips. The strength of the ash tree strips is in the layers of each year's growth and with the grain.

A white or black (brown) ash tree should be eleven feet long and at least six inches in diameter at the top, about ten to fifteen years of the sapwood. With an increment borer, we get a plug 1½ inch deep on the east side of the tree to find out how the tree has been growing. The plug is taken out at a 90-degree angle to the tree at about 4 feet high. This is the first step for testing the tree.

Step 1: Put hollow drill bit and handle together.
Step 2: Screw into the tree clockwise at 90° angle.
Step 3: Stick in 'ᴖ' shaped scoop.
Step 4: Twist handle counterclockwise half a turn making the 'ᴖ' into a 'ᴗ'.
Step 5: Pull out scoop with plug.

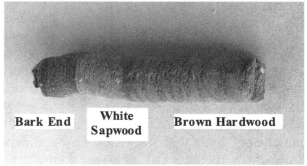

Bark End   **White Sapwood**   **Brown Hardwood**

The sapwood of black ash is white and the heartwood is dark brown. The more thick white rings found under the bark, the better the tree is growing. The length of the plug should be one and half inches, what is needed for the strips of the frame. This plug does not hurt the tree; it will fill in with time. It is after examining a tree carefully that we cut it. (In the old days, an axe was used to make a small notch to see the growth. The tree was tested and left standing if it was not growing well. We find some of these trees at times.

Once the tree is down, we measure about 11 feet for the first cut for the longest snowshoes. That length will be good for any type of snowshoes.

The second cut is made 12 to 16 inches long. This firewood length piece will be used to see if the tree will bend green for snowshoes or if it can be pounded for baskets. This is also a test of flexibility. For another test, the piece is split to get a strip the same size as the thickness of a snowshoe and forced around a round object about the same size as the front of the snowshoe. If the strip bends well, the tree will be good for snowshoes. If it cannot bend well, it is used for other purposes. That is the final test before we use the tree. (Note: Black ash that is grown in swamps with cedar trees and other evergreens do not seem to bend as well as ash trees that grow in clusters with other ash trees. It also seems that, the higher up in elevation that the tree grows, the less pliable it is.)

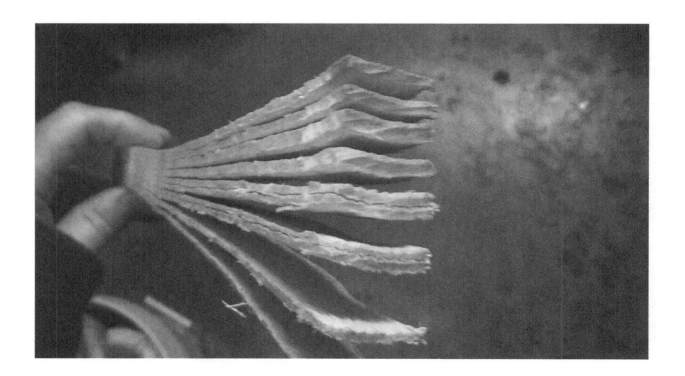

We have found that the tree bends better the closer you are to the stump or butt end. If a tree cannot be used for snowshoes, we test to see if it can be used for basket making. If not, we have it sawed into beautiful grained lumber that can be used for crosspieces and racks. All the time, we are careful not to damage the outside of the tree. The  remaining parts of the tree go into firewood. We prefer to cut our trees in November close to the time we will be using them. We can usually bury them in snow with a tarp on them to keep them from drying.

Cutting Wood Strips

Remember that you may need help to get a big tree out of the woods and into the work place. We have eliminated steaming the wood that was used for making the frames by selecting trees that bend green. We have also eliminated the tedious way the old timers used to split the tree to get the strips of wood to make the frames. We have kept the same principle they used of making the outside of the tree the outside of the snowshoe frame. We use the table saw to shape  the frames, because it is faster than the shaving horse and hand-draw shaver.

Once the tree is back at your workshop, place the tree at a comfortable height off the floor on rounded short sawhorse, * shaped top sawhorse that has been prepared in advance. Taking the strips off the tree is done preferably on a cold morning, when the tree is partially frozen. We use a radial saw (skill saw) for this job, and it seems the blade does not gum as much if the tree is frozen. It also keeps the blade cool.

With a drawknife, remove about half the thickness of the bark for a four-inch wide strip on top of the tree to check for knots or other defects. The bark that is left remaining will keep the strips from drying once they are off the tree.  (Note: Keep in mind that the outside around of the tree will be the outside of the snowshoe. A little bark should show up on the outside of the snowshoe.)

The lighter white sapwood growth rings go around the outside of frames. Split the tree to get the frame strips off once it has been saw cut around the outside of the log. A log that is six inches in diameter at the top will produce at least twelve strips for six pairs of snowshoes. If there is an increment borer hole or knot in the tree, start the first cut right next to it.

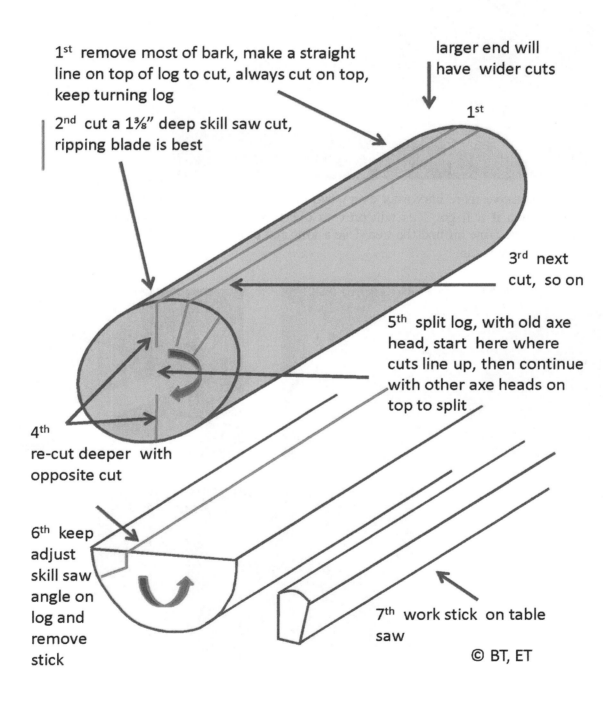

1st remove most of bark, make a straight line on top of log to cut, always cut on top, keep turning log

2nd cut a 1⅜" deep skill saw cut, ripping blade is best

larger end will have wider cuts

1st

3rd next cut, so on

5th split log, with old axe head, start here where cuts line up, then continue with other axe heads on top to split

4th re-cut deeper with opposite cut

6th keep adjust skill saw angle on log and remove stick

7th work stick on table saw

© BT, ET

61

Throw a line if the tree is straight or just stay on top of the tree with the skill saw. Always start from the top sawing towards the butt of the tree, cutting 1⅜ inches deep. After the first cut, turn the tree slightly to make a second cut 1¼ inches from the first cut at the top. Turn the tree after every cut to stay on top of the tree. (Remember the butt end diameter of the log is always greater.) Remove more bark after every two cuts to give the saw a break. Never push the saw to go faster than it will go. This will prevent overheating. You keep cutting, peeling, and turning until you have gone around the tree. Use a long flat chisel to help pull snowshoe frame strips off following the saw cut.

Continue around the log until finished. The log is now ready to be split in two. It is easier to start at the top of the log and make a second half inch deeper cut in the same two cuts where you will start splitting the log. Start the split at the top of the log with a thin ax head or wedge. As the split opens, use other wood wedges made of 2 inches by 4 inches, 12 inches long. Also, an old axe head or metal wedges can be used until there are two split pieces of the log. It is easy now to remove the strips off the open half log with the skill saw. Be careful not to cut too deep. This may damage the strip under the one being taken off. Make needed adjustments as to depth and angle as you go along.

The depth and the angle of the skill saw may have to slightly change as you move from the inside of the half log. The more strips that are done, the easier to learn how to set the blade and how to pass the saw. (The inside can be used for baskets, making big trees more useful.) Mark the strips in pairs as they are taken off because adjacent strips will be similar. Removing strips from a log takes about one hour. Some other tools, such as a small axe to cut the strands holding the tree together, may be needed to help remove the strips off the half logs. Be careful not to spoil the wood. The tree has to be green and not frozen to split it. Grain, which might run out every which way, will make you lose some strips. (Use steel toe boots for protection when working with a log, chainsaw, or any sharp tool that may drop on to your foot.)

Cover the strips that are not used at once in the winter snow until needed. A plastic sheet should be placed over the strips to hold the moisture in the wood under the snow. A tarp works well to keep the sunlight off. Use the working strips right away. Working with three pairs of snowshoes at a time is usually the fastest and most efficient way to make snowshoes. Hopefully, three molds are available to put them on. As the strips are made, put them on the molds right away.

Shaping the Wood Strips

Shaping two strips into snowshoe frames to be placed on the mold for drying is done by removing what is left of the bark with a drawknife. Be careful not to damage the wood since this is the side that will be on the outside of the frame where the pressure will be applied when bending around the mold. The table saw is used to do the entire cutting. Practice cuts and use great care when working with saws. Follow safety instructions. Find the straightest side of the strip for the first cut on the outside of the saw from the spacing fence and keep the bark side on the table. When cutting the strips, avoid the knots or bad spots. The shorter pieces can be used for smaller snowshoes when cut before the knots.

Do not worry if a strip is not too straight. Just remove a small amount of wood with each cut until you get proficient. Next turn the strip around with the bark side on top to finish squaring off that same side, still on same side of the saw. A jig made of three-quarter inch plywood is needed to fit on top of your table saw fence. That will keep you away from the fence and allow you to square off the other side of the strip. Even if the strip is not straight, the jig should be about two inches long and one and a half inches thick. It should be placed exactly on the side of the saw blades. Keep hands away from the fence and saw blade. When measuring for the size of your snowshoe frame, measure from the jig to the saw blade. Sand the strips, squaring them off. Once the two strips have been squared off to the same size, you are ready to shape the frames. We have made a chart that we have near the table saw with the measurements that we need for every type of snowshoes that we make. We will prepare the two strips for a pair of large cross-country snowshoes.

Holding the strips side-by-side with the outside of the frames in the same direction, make a center mark where the front end will be and also mark at ⅜ inch to show how thick the front tip is going to be. Make a mark at 13½ inch from the center mark to show where to start removing the wood on the inside of the front of the frames to the ⅜ inch mark at the center. Make a mark from the center mark 38½ inches on the frame to show where you will start cutting the wood at

the tail end. Turn the strips to make the same marks on the other side of the strips.

The 13½ inch mark is the distance from the center mark to start narrowing on the table saw to the ⅜ inch center mark. All cutting to shape the frame has to be done on the outside of the saw away from the fence and opposite of the bark side of the frame. The end cut is started at ⅜ inch until about 11 inches from the 38½ inch mark where the cut tapers out. Turn the strip to cut the other end and the other center cut. Remember the outside growth rings of the tree should go around the outside of your snowshoes without cuts or damage. The continuous growth rings make snowshoes stronger and less likely to break when bending them. Strips may not be perfectly straight but when you put them on the mold, they will be straightened out.

Once the strips are shaped on the table saw, remove any rough spots or bumps with a grinder using coarse sand paper. Do not sand on the bark side of the strip, which will be the outside of the snowshoes. The strips are now ready to be put on the mold. When waiting a few days, wrap strips in plastic to keep them from drying. Keep all parts together so they are easy to find. Numbering of all parts on the same mold can help to keep you organized. The wedges

could be made to stay together with the mold. Even the small strips of ash wood used to protect the frame should be kept together on the mold. A box could be made to hold all the parts needed to save time. Keep pieces with the same markings together. Mark all the snowshoe strips, even the side that comes off the mold so you will know all information. If one frame breaks or gets damaged, keep it as a spare.

Placing Frames on the Mold

Before putting the strips on the mold, pre-bend them, to make them more pliable, one stick at a time over a barrel with a log on top. Do this up to twenty times moving a little over the center of the stick where it bends. (The tails of the green mountain snowshoe would also need to be pre-bent.)

Bending Around the Mold

Our molds are made for one pair of snowshoes at the same time. To start, place the mold on its side on a small platform about 6 inches high to make it easier to work. This does not need

to be too wide but 2 feet and 3 feet long to keep firmly in place, with enough room to work the strips around the mold. Place two strips on the mold so the center mark on strips will be close to the center mark on the front end of the mold. Use five inch spikes and wooden wedges to hold the strips tight on the top side of the mold. To start bending the strips on the front of the mold, we use a c-clamp where the wood is thicker on the strips using a hole in the mold. Turn the mold with the strips on the other side and finish turning the strips one at a time and wedge them tightly. To bend the long tail ends in place, we have a wooden invention with a two ton hydraulic jack for that job.

(The old timers used a 6 foot plank three inches thick and ten inches wide with two series of holes four inches apart half-way through the plank and large enough to hold ¾ inch galvanized pipes that were four feet long. We also used this method when we first started. The mold with the strips would be placed on the plank with the tails over the series of holes where the pipes could be used to pry the tail ends in place. The holes should be slightly larger than the diameter of the pipes. We used a cut piece of plywood with a notch the size to fit over the tails and the mold to hold everything in place when removing the pipes.)

Wrap the two strips and wedge them as you go around the form (mold). The two ends are set bottom-to-bottom (back-to-back) on the same form. Place two strips on the mold and wedge them tight. We use 5-inch spikes and wooden wedges for that purpose. To start the bending in front around the mold where the wood strips are thicker, we have a hole in the mold to place a c-clamp to bend that section of the strip that is the hardest part of the frame to bend. Now turn the mold to the other side and finish turning the strips around the front end and wedging them tight.

Closing and Tail Ends

Snowshoe frames with tails are tied in a more traditional way. To shape the tails, we have made a wooden invention where we can use a 2-ton hydraulic jack. It squeezes the ends together, giving shape to the snowshoe and keeping the tail end straight.

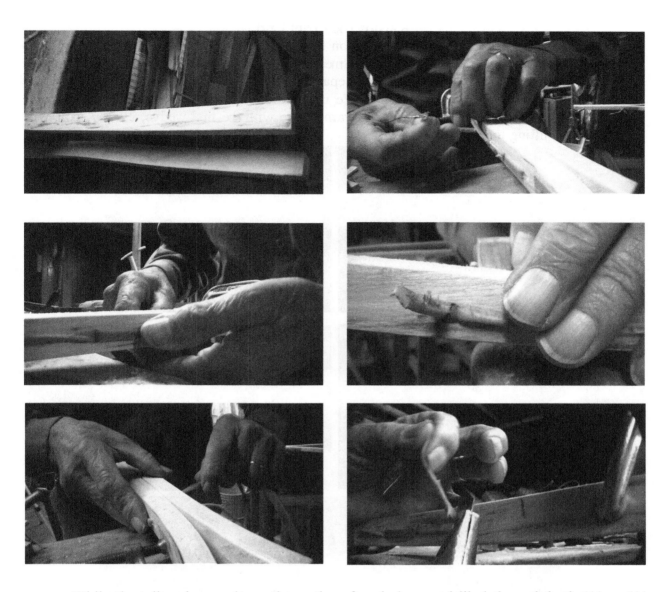

While the tail ends are clamped together, four holes are drilled through both 1½ or 1¼ inches apart. The first hole is $\frac{5}{32}$ inch, the second and third $\frac{7}{23}$ inch and the last is ¼ inch, 1 inch from the end. A two-foot length of smaller rawhide is passed through the front hole half way, next both ends are passed through the next two holes from the opposite sides. At the last hole, just one end goes through the hole and around the rawhide on the other side then back through the same hole to the other side. A pair of pliers is used to put pressure on the end on the other side until that end is forced half way in the larger hole. The ends are cut off and once dried, the locked rawhide holds the snowshoe tail together without the use of metal.

(Tails used to be nailed or bolted together. Now we tie them together with rawhide to eliminate any metal on our snowshoes.)

Raising the Front End

Where you will be applying pressure on the frames, use ⊠ inch thick strips of wood to protect them. To turn up the front of the frames, place the mold with the frames flat on the platform. With two large screw drivers, start separating the frames in front of the mold until the frames are about one inch above the mold. We use a wooden tool, a 16 x ½ x ½ inch stick, to turn up the front of the frames. Now lift the frame more with the first wedge, 2½ x 7 inch, with the help of the lifting tool.

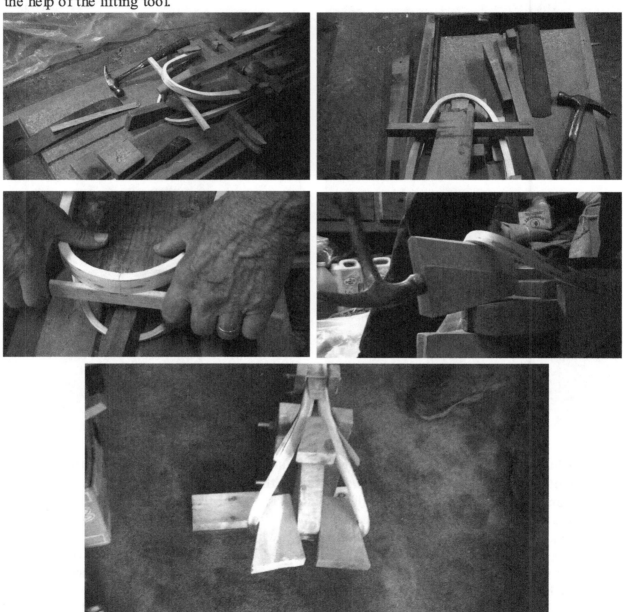

There is a tool we made to raise the front end with this on both sides of the center. This wooden tool is made of ¾ inch thick maple, 2¾ inches wide and 20¼ inches long. One end has a 1¾ inch slot in the center that is 2½ inches deep and the other end is shaped as a handle. The outside of the two prongs are rounded. With a block of ¾ inches maple, 2¾ x 4 inches, another block is used for leverage as we pry the front end up enough with the two prong tool to insert a wedge block. Use another block, ¾ x 2 x 5 inches next, for more leverage.

As the large cross country frame is turned up (check diagram of wedge for each type of mold), we insert a wedge block of wood made of 1½ inches thick wood, 7 inches long, 2½ inches high at one end and 5½ inches high at the other with the top slightly rounded. The 2½ inches end is inserted between the two prongs of the leverage tool, between the frame being raised and the mold. After one frame has been turned up, the mold is turned over on the platform and the other frame is turned up with another block inserted to hold the frame while drying.

We have found that black ash bends better when turning the front ends up, providing there are no defects in the wood. The wood should be green and not dried. If you are making snowshoes for a person weighing over 200 pounds, use thicker wood. If the wood you are using is harder to turn up, turn both snowshoe frames about 3 inches on the mold, then use a wedge ¾ inches thick and 4½ inches long, one end ½ inches high and the other 3½ inches high. These wedges are placed between the front sides of the frames on the mold and hammered in to help turn up the thick part of the frames.

The front ends of the snowshoe are turned up before drying 5 feet over the stove for ten to eleven days. Keep moving the wedge in with a hammer a bit every day about ½ inch to 1 inch if it is hard to bend right off. After ten to eleven days of drying, the frames are taken off the forms when loose. We have made a rack to keep the snowshoe frames in place once removed off the mold until needed for the next process. Rack: For LCC (large cross country) snowshoes the spreader is a piece of wood: 13½" x ¾" x ¼", [for LGM (large green mountain): 11" x ¾" x ¼", and for SCC (small cross country): 10¼" x ¾" x ¼".] It is placed between the top ends of two back-to-back snowshoe frames to keep the upward bend. The width of the snowshoes should be: 14" x ¾" x ¼" for the wider snowshoes, 13¼" x ¾" x ¼" for the average width, and 11½ " x ¾" x ¼" for the smaller width snowshoes. Put the snowshoes on a rack with a jig to keep the tips apart. The spreader rack consists of a piece of wood that has a V cut out of both ends. These spreader pieces hold the tips apart.

The second part of the rack is two pieces of wood with rounded head bolts holding the snowshoes back to back. This is used for storing after removing from mold and on the finished product. A notch is taken out of the holes at the end of the rack holding sticks to allow the ¼ inch bolt to slide in and out when loosened. These two pieces of wood should be fairly good quality. Place these racks first below the snowshoes crosspieces. Then slowly slide them up one side at a time until tight.

Next, place one of the spreader sticks on one of the snowshoe top tips, pull the other snowshoe tip until the spreader is in place, and hold the tips so that they do not move. Once the spreader is in place bring up the holding racks, two pieces of wood held by screws, one side at a time up until the top crosspiece area. This should press the snowshoes together until it is tight. (You may want to tie the tail of the Green Mountain snowshoes together with twine within a few days so it does not get out of shape.)

Bear Paws

Bear paws and modified bear paws are marked slightly different. The wood of the back ends of bear paws taper. These thinning pieces overlap at the end, with the finishing end longer. The center mark of the strip will have to be off-set to allow for the different lengths. Make adjustments depending on the molds so it is always started with a slightly longer measurement than required. With practice putting strips on molds, corrections can be made. Add these corrections to your card chart for each mold once the strips are shaped on the table saw. We take off any rough spots with an angle grinder. Coarse sandpaper works better on green wood.

Putting modified green mountain bear paws on the mold is different because of the back end. The small green mountain mold has a ¼ inch indentation where the short end of the strips are anchored (Large green mountain is ⅜ inch.). We use 2 inch screws in predrilled holes in the strips and mold where the indentation. Use a thin piece of metal to hold the strips in place. As pressure is applied with the mold on the side, start bending the strips around the mold past the front end and the back where the strips overlap. We have a tool we use to turn the strips over the anchored ends and to the other side, clamping the strips in place as we end.

This tool consists of two 37 inch strips of hard wood spaced apart slightly over the width of the thickness of the mold and opened at one end with a wooden roller bolted about 8 inches from the open ends. Holes are drilled one inch from the ends of the open ends and through the mold at a distance where, when a spike is inserted through the holes, the wooden roller will roll over the outside strips making it easy to clamp in holes in the mold as you roll around. The front ends of the frames are processed the same as regular snowshoe frames. Once dried, the overlapping back strips are tied by wrapping with a good heavy strip of rawhide.

The front ends of the frames of modified bear-paws are processed the same as regular snowshoe frames. Regular snowshoe frames with tails are tied in a more traditional way. A flex piece of metal, ⅛ inch by ¾ inch by 16 inch, taped on the front bend of the stick will help it out if it wants to split outward on you. Even if splits out a bit, you can sand and wrap rawhide over the front end to also help to protect the wood in the brush. The bear paws have holes in the molds to help with a tool to bend the frames around the mold. The tool works really well, fast and easy, which saves time. All the upper front hard wood wedge pieces are hammered in easily, a bit at a time. If it is hard to bend or easy to bend, just pound it in. You will also know when it is dry because the wooden wedges will want to fall out by themselves.

Placing the Crosspieces

After the back ends of the snowshoes are tied together, the crosspieces are put in place. Where the crosspiece is place is very important. For crosspieces, we use straight grain ash, a good ⅝ inches thick by 1¼ inches wide. Smaller wood frames use shorter crosspieces. The length will vary depending on the width of the frame. To mark the frame where the crosspieces will be, you set both frames, one on top of the other, making sure the tail ends are lined up. With a piece of wood stock laid across approximately where the front crosspieces will be, mark both frames on the same sides 15 inches from the tip of the frames and the back crosspieces 19¼ inches from the front ones. This 19¼ inches includes the width of the crosspieces. You mark both frames on the same side, front and back. Then you lift the top frame and turn the bottom frame upside down. You line up the back ends and sides. Now, mark the two other sides of the frames that are not marked. The crosspiece tool can also be used.

To measure the length of the front crosspiece, you put a spacer inside of the frame to where you want the width of the snowshoe to be. Place a piece of wood stock underneath the front markings on the frame and mark the wood on the inside of the frame, on one end, and the other end on the outside of the frame. Cut two pieces of that length for one pair of shoes. Bevel the ends of these pieces to fit the holes in the frame that will be 1 inch long and ¼ inch wide on the surface and ⅜ inch deep and ⅛ by 1 inch in the bottom. The crosspieces will have to be notched towards the center of the snowshoe to fit the one inch hole. You want the smallest hole possible in your frame to keep the crosspiece and the frame as strong and sturdy as possible.

To make the hole in the frame, we use three different size homemade chisels for the beveled sides and a one inch chisel for the long side. The homemade chisels are made from the handle ends of flat files. Larger ones are ⅝ inch wide for the first cut, the second ¼ inch and the third ⅛ inch. (Note: smaller frames do not use the ⅝ inch wide file.) It is easy to make the hole

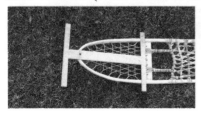 since you are just cutting out the growth rings of the tree. These are the same tools and the same techniques the old snowshoe makers used.

Drilling the Frame Holes

Marking the Holes (Half strip)	Marking Front End (balance holes)	Marking Front Crosspiece	Marking Back End	Marking Back Crosspiece (balance holes)
Large Cross-Country (LCC)	8 holes 1¼" from crosspiece 3½" next space 2" next six spaces ¾" to center mark 16 holes total	Center 7 holes one inch apart	6 holes 3" from crosspiece 2¼" between holes 12 holes total	Center 6 holes about one inch apart
Small Cross-Country (SCC)	8 holes 1" from crosspiece 2" next space 1½" next six spaces ⅝" to center mark 16 holes total	Center 7 holes one inch apart	6 holes 2¼" from crosspiece 1½" between holes 12 holes total	Center 6 holes about one inch apart
Large Green Mountain (LGM)	8 holes 1½" from crosspiece 2¾" next space 1¾" next six spaces ⅝" to center mark 16 holes total	Center 7 holes one inch apart	7 holes 1½" from crosspiece 2¾" next space 1¾" next five spaces ⅝" to center mark 14 holes total	Center 6 holes about one inch apart
Small Green Mountain (SGM)	8 holes 1" from crosspiece 1¾" next space 1½" next six spaces ½" to center mark 16 holes total	Center 7 holes one inch apart	5½ holes 1½" from crosspiece 1" next five spaces 1½ to center mark 11 holes total	Center 6 holes about one inch apart

Holes can be adjusted a bit to balance better.
** Double check all your marks before drilling.
© B T , E T

Drill Hole Spacer

--½ inch thick x ¾ inch wide x 2½ inches long hardwood
--Four holes, two sets of holes ½ inch apart from hole center, 1 inch between
sets (second set is spare)
--Work toward crosspiece using only two holes at a time.
--Center spacer along outside of frame

Once the crosspieces are in place, we mark the frames where the holes will be drilled. For that purpose, use strips of heavy paper or ¾ inch ribbons/stencils with holes that are different distances apart. Place the stencil pattern on the outside of the frame to make the marks. Before drilling, double check the snowshoe frames, back-to-back, so that the holes line up. Hold the pattern firmly on the frame to drill the holes. With a piece of hard wood that is the width of the thickness of the snowshoe frame, predrilled with holes for a guide, drill holes in the frames. Use a ⅛ inch drill bit that is sharp to make the holes. Once the holes are finished, use a utility knife to remove a small 'v' shaped section of the outside wood between the holes where the rawhide will be passed on the outside of the snowshoe. This is done before any weaving has started. Only ⅛-inch deep notch is needed. Try not to make it too deep. The part of the rawhide in this 'v' cut is to protect the rawhide and give a smoother finish. A rubber tire inner tube can be cut into two-inch wide circular piece to help hold the frame tight. This will hold the crosspiece in place. When crosspieces fall out, they may be lost. The snowshoe frames are now ready for the three-way weave with rawhide.

Earlier snowshoes had only one hole, instead of two, for the top and bottom parts of the snowshoe. The makers would pass the rawhide through the hole and put pieces of skin or fur (tuffs of moose) on the outside, passing the rawhide back through the same hole to continue with the weaving. When yarn came along, they used it to hold the rawhide to the frame. It made the snowshoes more colorful.

Drilling the Crosspieces.

The crosspiece length will dictate the spacing of the holes for its balance of the weaving. The number of holes needed are drilled in the right places. A hole-pattern on a strong ¾-inch ribbon can be used to cut the holes on the crosspiece. Line up the ribbon with the crosspieces. Use a scrap piece of hard wood under the crosspieces if it is done with a hand drill. This way, the wood hole will not splinter out when drilling the holes in the crosspieces. A

drill press works best if you want a clean hole and you do not plan to finish them right away. You may stamp a logo on the crosspiece if desired. A number can also be put on the tails.

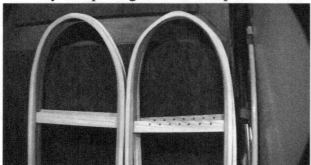 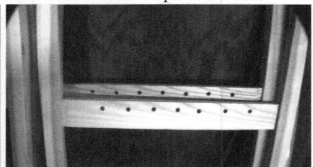

Tips

1. White ash can make thinner frames than black ash because it is stronger and heavier.
2. Test the top 16-inch piece of wood ½" x ½" x 16" to a bend test over a round block or on a barrel.
3. Testing one pair of strips is usually a good indicator for the quality of the entire tree.
4. Keep extra strips of wood out in the cold. Cover them with plastic and do not let them get dry.
5. Keep the strips marked and side-by-side. Matching strips make better-looking pairs of snowshoes.
6. Mark the butt of the tree because it bends the best for some snowshoe frames (bear paws).
7. You should get enough trees in the fall to last you for snowshoe making throughout the winter.
8. Get trees that are not damaged by heavy equipment. If you are having a skidder move the log, leave the tree longer and have them grab the tree by the top so it does not touch the part you need for snowshoes.
9. Do not drag the tree in the mud because it will dull the saw blade when cutting the strips of the log.
10. The band saw can also be used for cutting the strips into shape and may even be faster than the table saw. A few jigs may be used to help the process.

Notes:

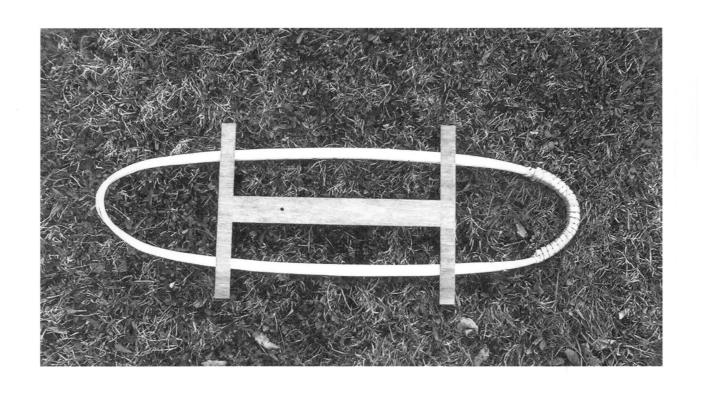

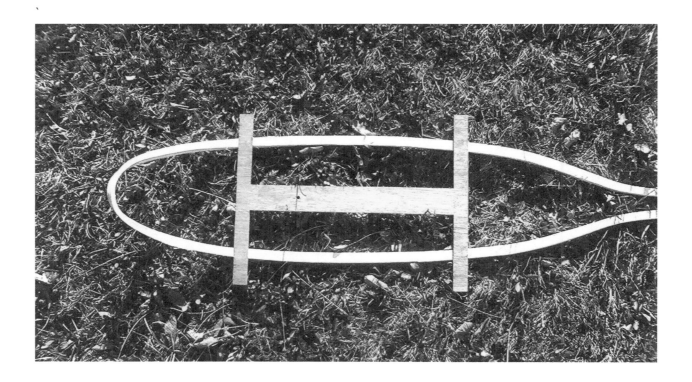

Large Green Mountain and Large Cross Country

Centering Crosspiece Tool
place where the crosspieces go and mark to cut out

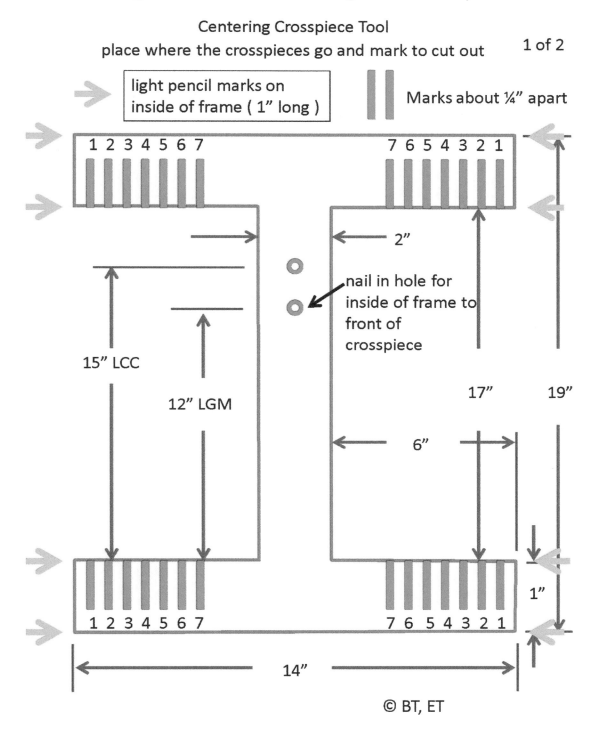

light pencil marks on
inside of frame (1" long)

Marks about ¼" apart

1 2 3 4 5 6 7   7 6 5 4 3 2 1

2"

nail in hole for
inside of frame to
front of
crosspiece

15" LCC

12" LGM

17"   19"

6"

1"

1 2 3 4 5 6 7   7 6 5 4 3 2 1

14"

© BT, ET

Small Cross Country and Small Green Mountain

Centering Crosspiece Tool
place where the crosspieces go and mark to cut out

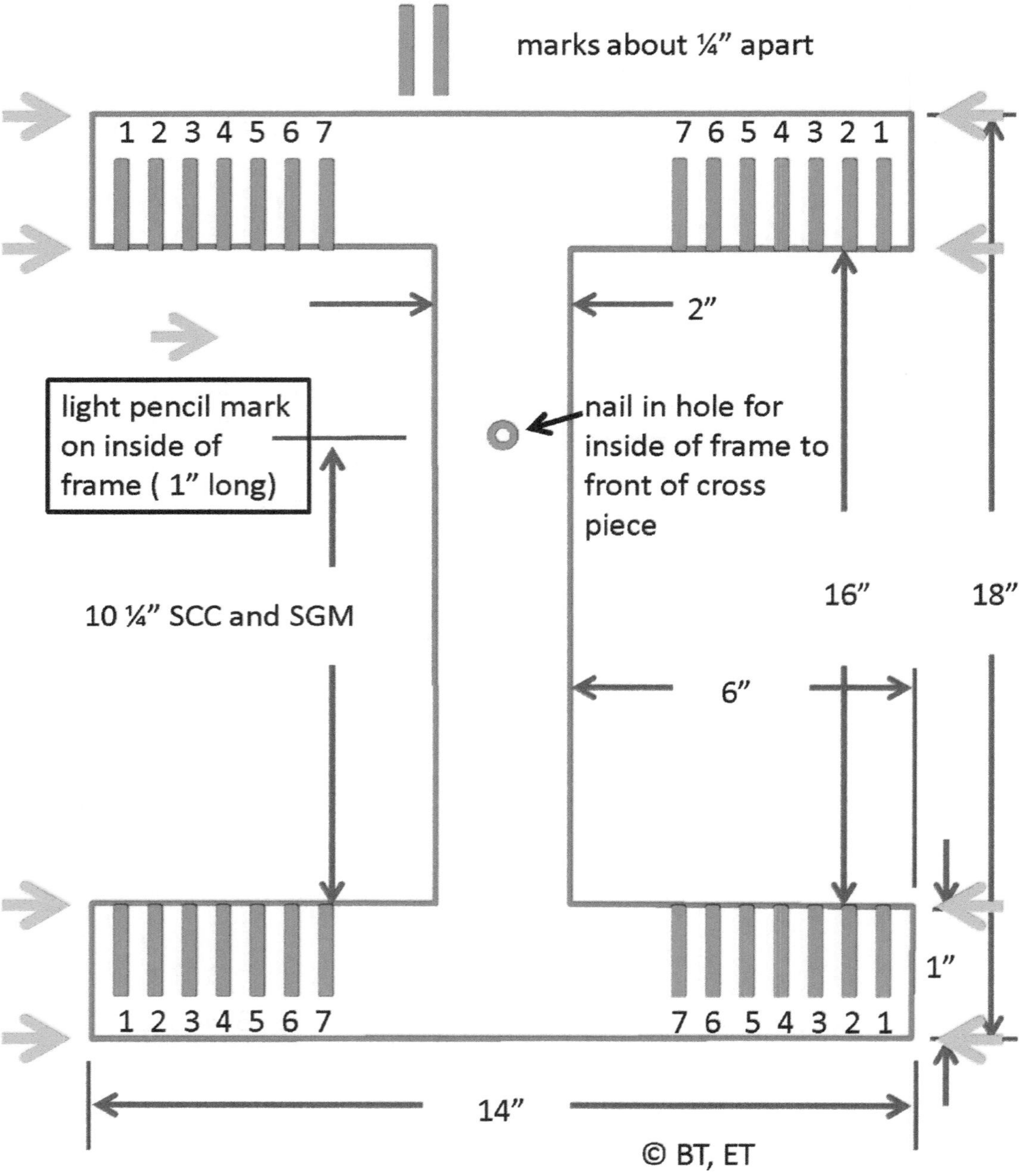

marks about ¼" apart

1 2 3 4 5 6 7   7 6 5 4 3 2 1

2"

light pencil mark
on inside of
frame (1" long)

nail in hole for
inside of frame to
front of cross
piece

10 ¼" SCC and SGM

16"   18"

6"

1 2 3 4 5 6 7   7 6 5 4 3 2 1

1"

14"

© BT, ET

tool for helping with the front end

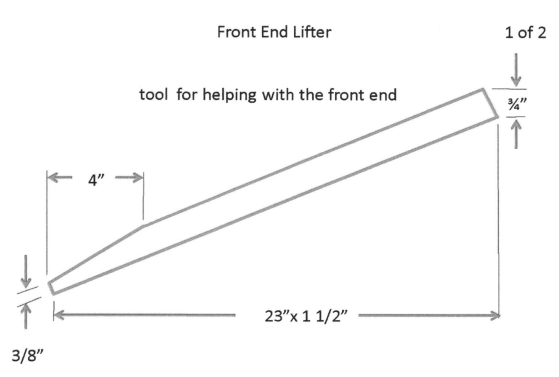

¾"

4"

23"x 1 1/2"

3/8"

first stick to start with to lift the front end of the frame

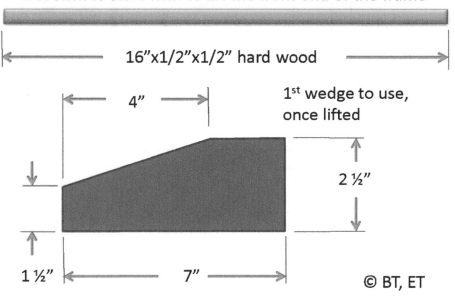

16"x1/2"x1/2" hard wood

4"

1st wedge to use, once lifted

2 ½"

1 ½"

7"

© BT, ET

All-Types Of Frame Front End Lifting Tools

use the right wedge with the mold pattern

step 1 1-4, step 2 2-4, sliding 3 wedge in place

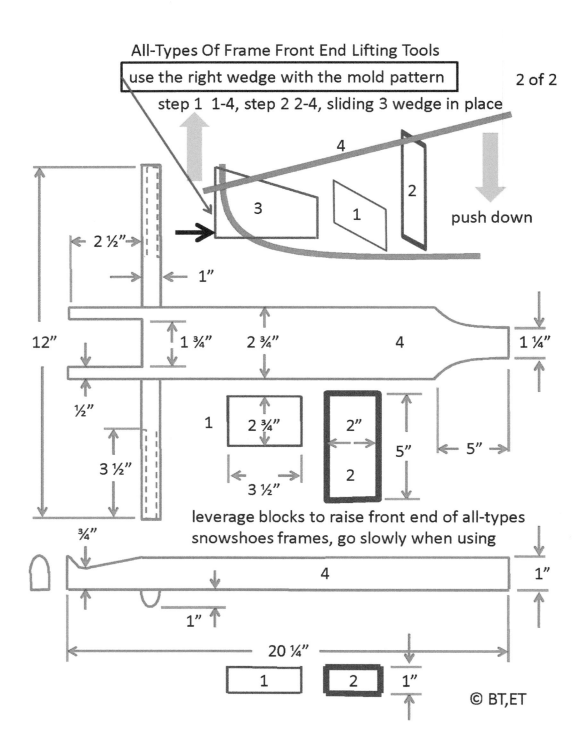

push down

leverage blocks to raise front end of all-types snowshoes frames, go slowly when using

© BT,ET

all ¾" thick hard wood, glued and pre-drilled, screwed together except for one moving part

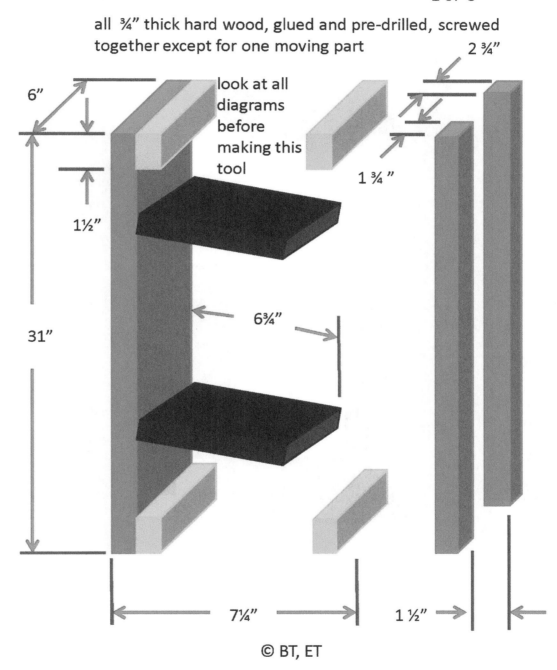

look at all diagrams before making this tool

6"

1½"

31"

6¾"

2 ¾"

1 ¾ "

7¼"

1 ½"

© BT, ET

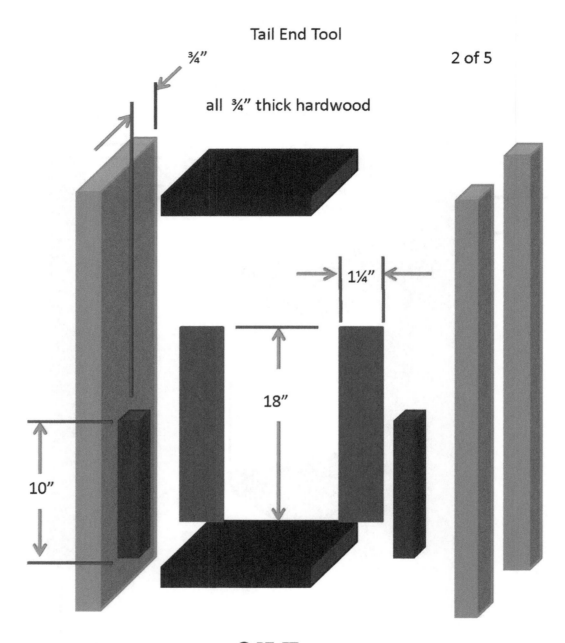

all ¾" thick hardwood

© BT, ET

Tail End Tool

all ¾" thick hardwood if not marked

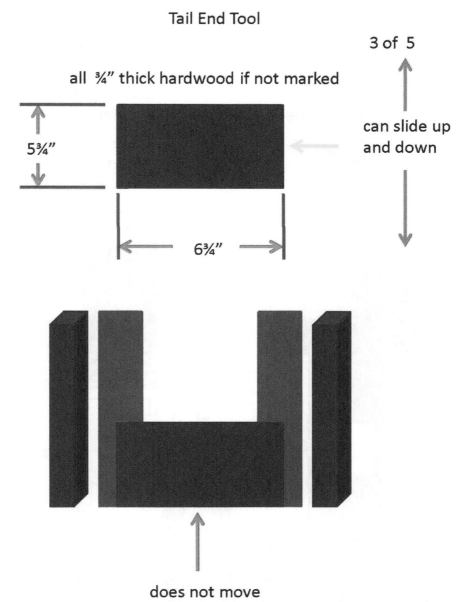

5¾"

6¾"

can slide up
and down

does not move

all wooden parts are glued , pre-drill, and screwed together

© BT, ET

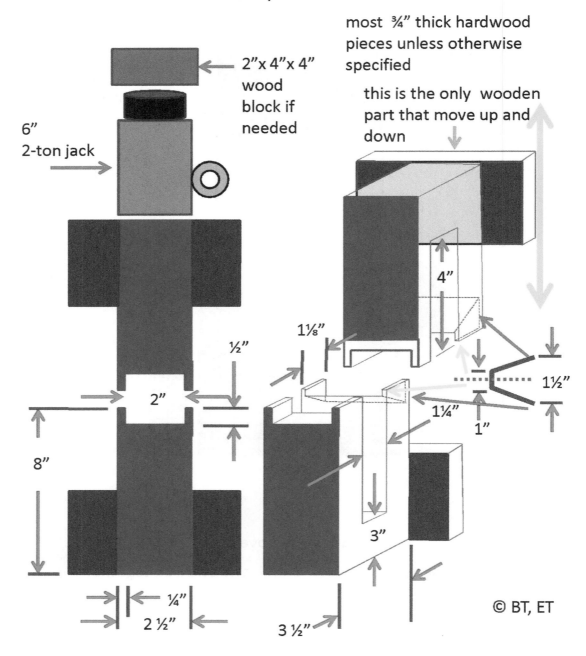

most ¾" thick hardwood
pieces unless otherwise
specified

this is the only wooden
part that move up and
down

2"x 4"x 4"
wood
block if
needed

6"
2-ton jack

½"

2"

8"

1⅛"

4"

1½"

1¼"

1"

3"

¼"

2 ½"

3 ½"

© BT, ET

86

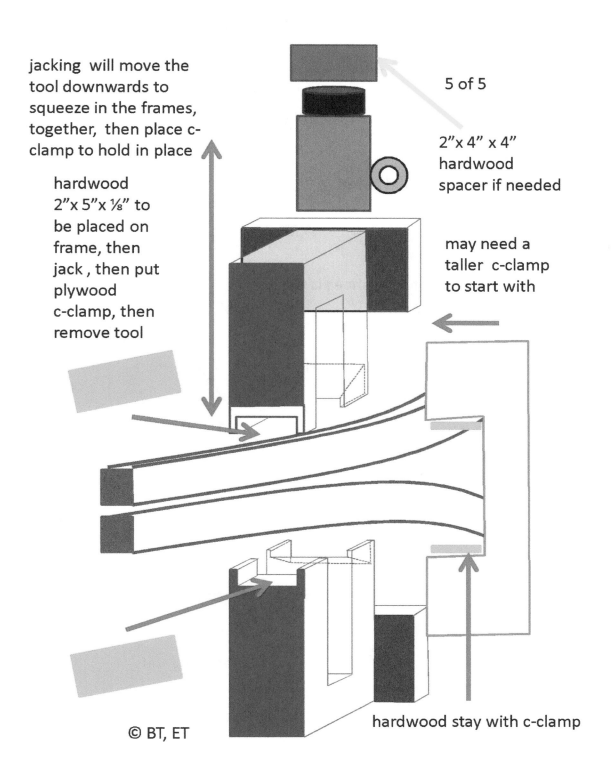

jacking will move the tool downwards to squeeze in the frames, together, then place c-clamp to hold in place

hardwood 2"x 5"x ⅛" to be placed on frame, then jack, then put plywood c-clamp, then remove tool

2"x 4" x 4" hardwood spacer if needed

may need a taller c-clamp to start with

hardwood stay with c-clamp

© BT, ET

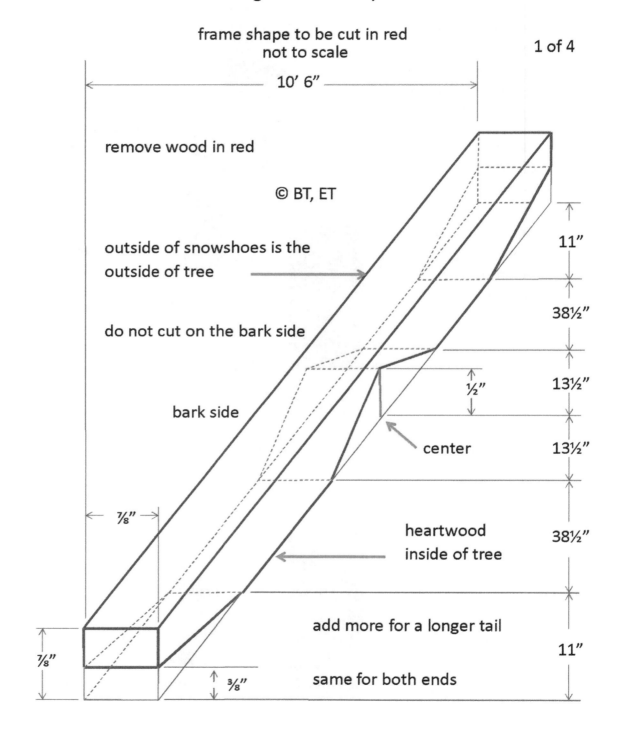

frame shape to be cut in red
not to scale

10' 6"

remove wood in red

© BT, ET

outside of snowshoes is the
outside of tree

do not cut on the bark side

bark side

center

heartwood
inside of tree

add more for a longer tail

same for both ends

11"

38½"

13½"

13½"

38½"

11"

½"

⅞"

⅞"

⅜"

frame shape to be cut in red
not to scale

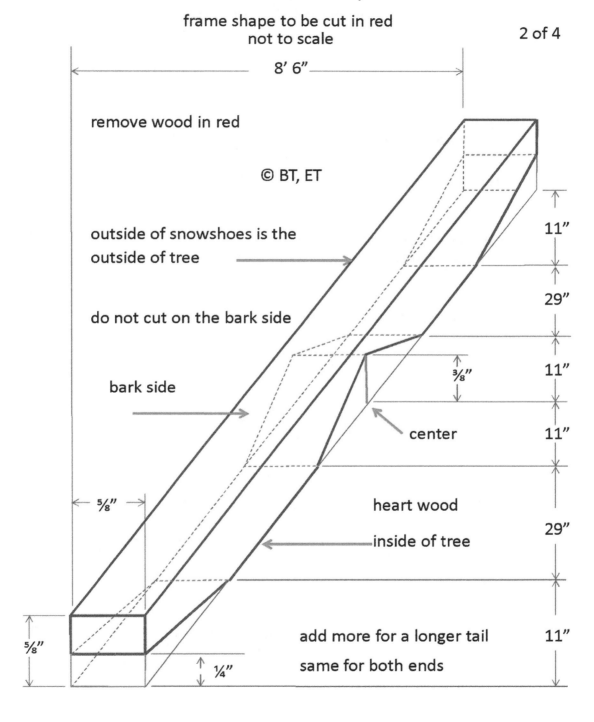

8' 6"

remove wood in red

© BT, ET

outside of snowshoes is the
outside of tree

do not cut on the bark side

bark side

11"

29"

11"

⅜"

center

11"

heart wood

inside of tree

29"

⅝"

add more for a longer tail

same for both ends

11"

⅝"

¼"

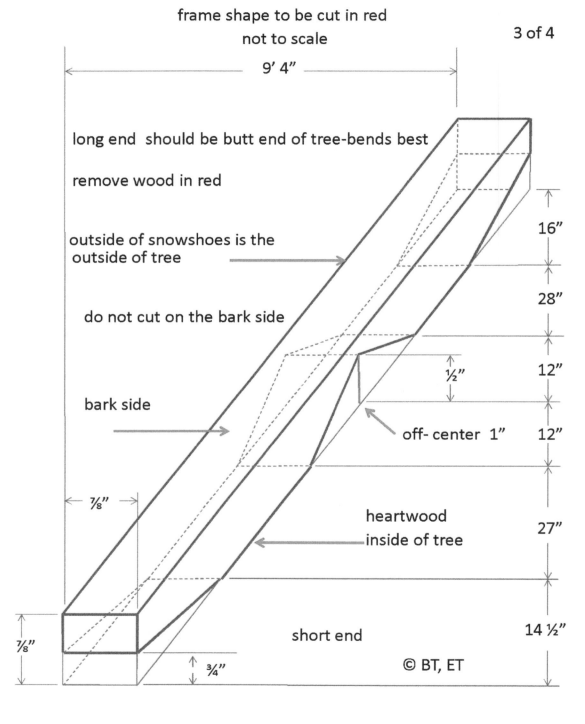

Large Green Mountain Modified

frame shape to be cut in red

not to scale

9' 4"

long end should be butt end of tree-bends best

remove wood in red

outside of snowshoes is the
outside of tree

do not cut on the bark side

bark side

⅞"

16"

28"

½"   12"

off- center 1"   12"

heartwood
inside of tree   27"

short end   14 ½"

⅞"

¾"

© BT, ET

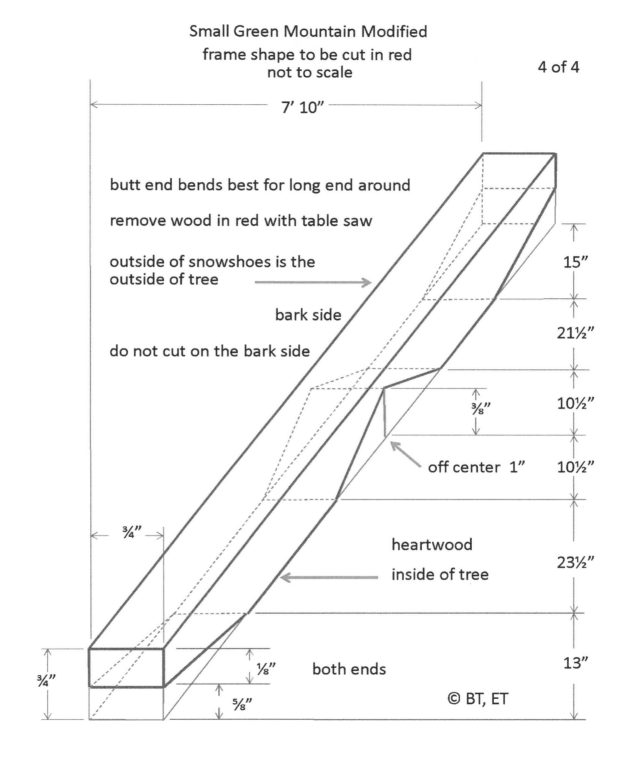

Small Green Mountain Modified
frame shape to be cut in red
not to scale

7' 10"

butt end bends best for long end around

remove wood in red with table saw

outside of snowshoes is the
outside of tree

bark side

do not cut on the bark side

15"

21½"

3/8"

10½"

off center 1"   10½"

heartwood

inside of tree

23½"

3/4"

13"

1/8"   both ends

3/4"

5/8"

© BT, ET

Tying ends LCC and SCC

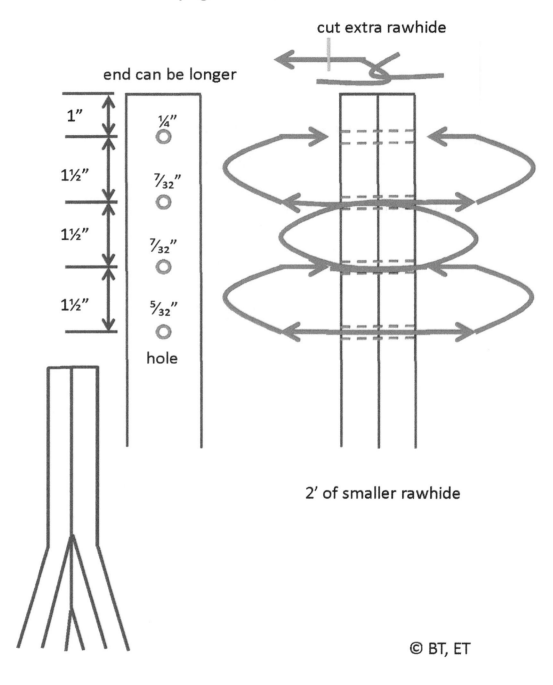

cut extra rawhide

end can be longer

1"

1/4"

1 1/2"

7/32"

1 1/2"

7/32"

1 1/2"

5/32"

hole

2' of smaller rawhide

© BT, ET

Back end Large and Small Green Mountain Roll Around Tool

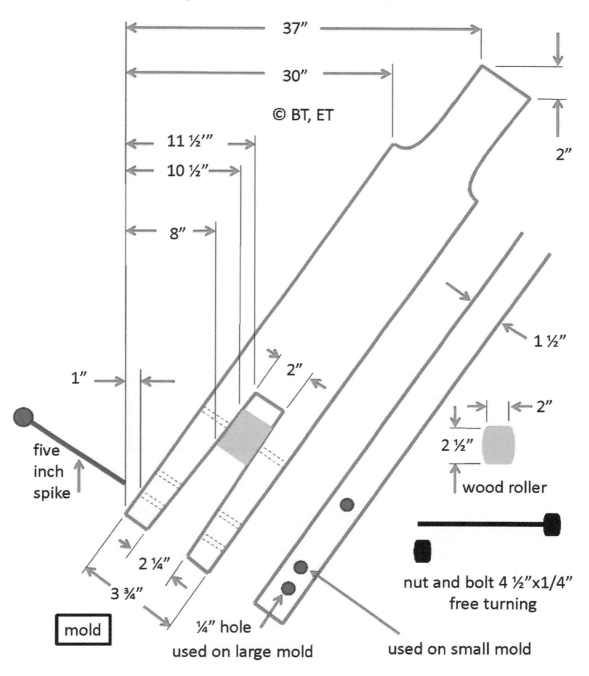

37"

30"

© BT, ET

11 ½'"

10 ½"

8"

2"

2"

1"

1 ½"

2"

2 ½"

wood roller

five
inch
spike

2 ¼"

3 ¾"

nut and bolt 4 ½"x1/4"
free turning

mold

¼" hole
used on large mold

used on small mold

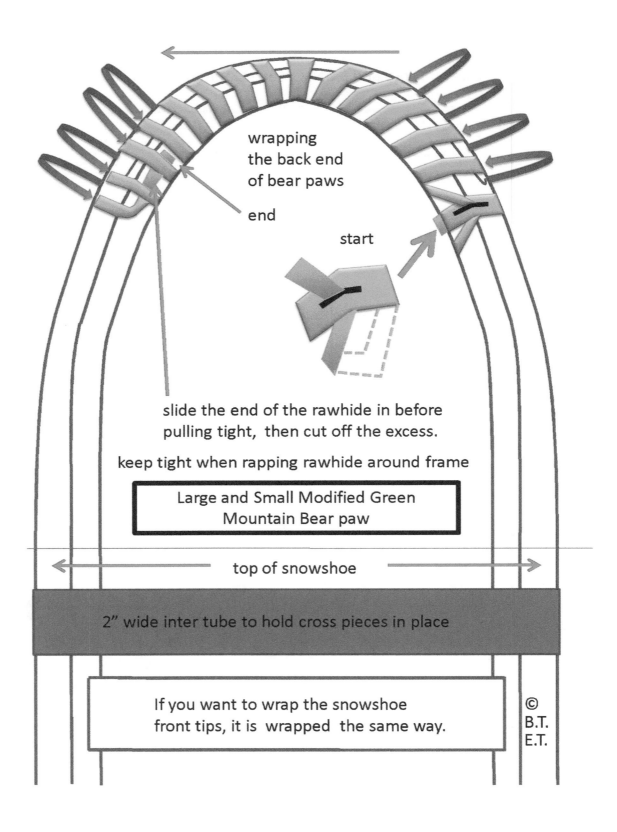

wrapping
the back end
of bear paws

end

start

slide the end of the rawhide in before
pulling tight, then cut off the excess.

keep tight when rapping rawhide around frame

**Large and Small Modified Green
Mountain Bear paw**

top of snowshoe

2" wide inter tube to hold cross pieces in place

If you want to wrap the snowshoe
front tips, it is wrapped the same way.

© B.T. E.T.

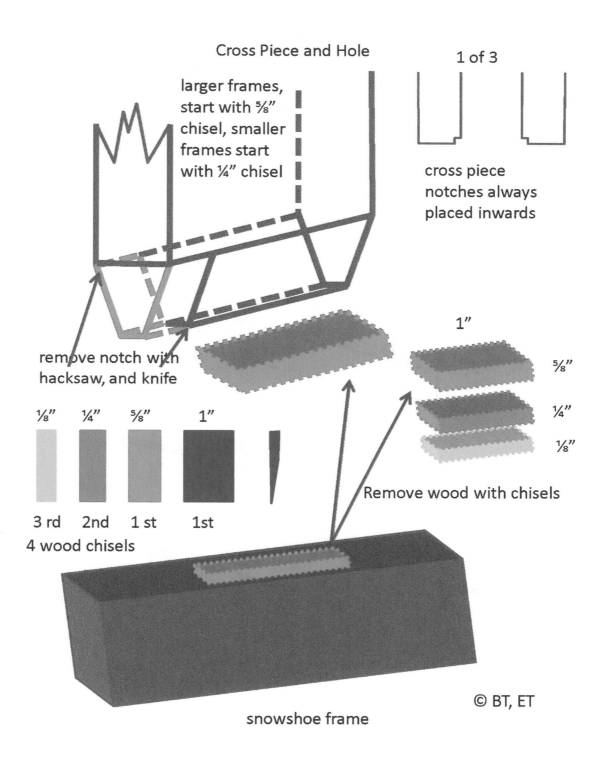

Cross Piece and Hole

larger frames, start with ⅝" chisel, smaller frames start with ¼" chisel

cross piece notches always placed inwards

remove notch with hacksaw, and knife

⅛" ¼" ⅝" 1"

3 rd 2nd 1 st 1st

4 wood chisels

1"

⅝"

¼"

⅛"

Remove wood with chisels

snowshoe frame

© BT, ET

95

Cross Piece and Hole

large snowshoe frames and large cross pieces only

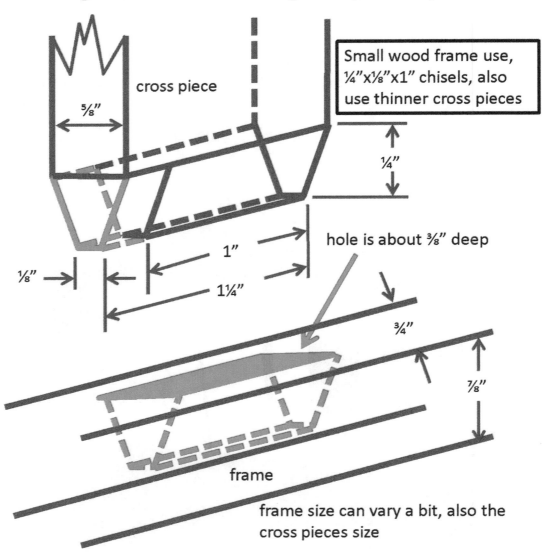

cross piece

5/8"

Small wood frame use, ¼"x⅛"x1" chisels, also use thinner cross pieces

¼"

hole is about ⅜" deep

⅛"

1"

1¼"

¾"

⅞"

frame

frame size can vary a bit, also the cross pieces size

no glue, you want the cross piece to move a bit in hole

© BT, ET

Cross Piece and Hole

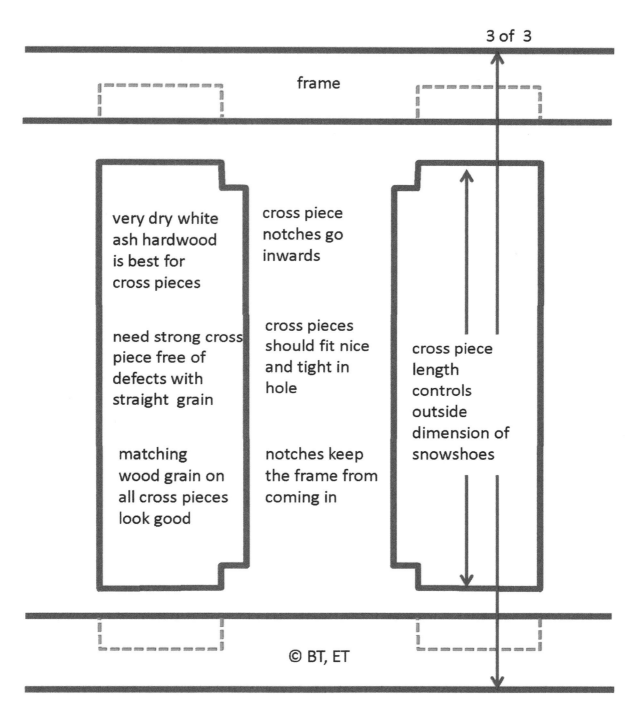

frame

very dry white
ash hardwood
is best for
cross pieces

cross piece
notches go
inwards

need strong cross
piece free of
defects with
straight grain

cross pieces
should fit nice
and tight in
hole

cross piece
length
controls
outside
dimension of
snowshoes

matching
wood grain on
all cross pieces
look good

notches keep
the frame from
coming in

© BT, ET

Notes:

Chapter 6 - Rawhide

Jordan Theriault

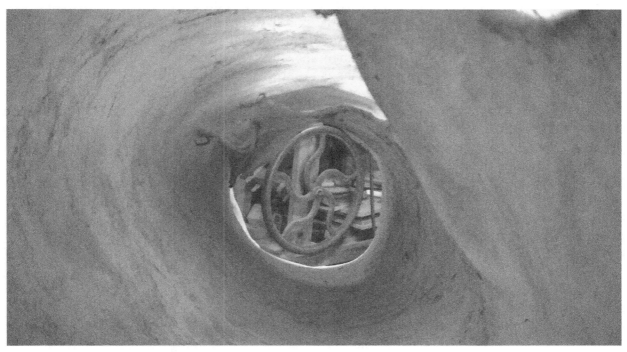

Before the snowshoes are ready to lace, you will need to prepare your rawhide. Rawhide is made from a cow or bull skin. (Deer and moose are too stretchy. They are harder to cut, work with, and do not work well. Beaver rawhide may repel water, but it is not as strong as cowhide.) Cattle hides make the best rawhide because they are thick and can be pre-stretched before lacing. Then, there is no further stretching. As the weaving dries, the rawhide will pull the frame in very tight, which is very important for good working snowshoes.

Getting a Cow Skin

The best time to look for a cow is in the fall, or early spring, when the skin has a good thickness and a better quality. Big animals in the summer are also good because they are not so thick. Big bull skins are not too good for rawhide because the skin is thick, and it weighs more. (Farmers, prior to electricity, would butcher their animals in early December when the snow brought the cold weather.) Now, we can get hides just about any  time, so we prepare the rawhide early in the spring or fall when there are fewer bugs and cooler weather. Hides can only be kept dried, salted, or frozen.

Most of time, you need to know what you are going to do with the skin of rawhide ahead of time. At least, try to save the thick part of the skin if you have to take care of the skin quickly. There will always be a lot of small rawhide on the other skins that you get. On average, one cow skin will make about five to seven pairs of snowshoes worthy of rawhide webbing.

The first place to look for cow skins is at farms in the area where you live that butcher their own stock. It is a good idea to have contact with various cow farmers ahead of time. This is the best way that I have found to purchase skins at a reasonable price. Several farmers may need to be contacted before you begin your project to see when the skins will become available. When getting a cow skin, both cow and bull are okay. Holstein types of cows are best. It is important to explain to the skinner of the rawhide that you prefer that the skins do not have cuts in them. Inspect the skin before making the final purchase. Even if it might cost extra for a good skin, it is worth it if it is free of too many cuts. To ensure that the skin will be unmarred, tell the skinner that it is okay to leave some fat or meat. The person skinning the hide needs to be careful and know your requirements beforehand.

Occasionally one of these farmers may contact you when they have a dead cow and want to give it to you. Some years, when there is no market for hides, you can get hides for nothing, since they are throwing them away. We prefer working the hide fresh. Skin the cow immediately in the summer months and within a day or so in the winter months, as long as the cow is kept in a cold place. If you have to wait for some time before using the hide, fold the hide hair out and freeze it. A freezer can be used to keep the rawhide frozen until it is needed. It may take 15 minutes or so to thaw, depending on the temperature. It is always a good idea to get a few cow skins at a time, because doing a lot of skins ahead of time gives you a good supply to work with and to choose from for different parts of the snowshoe. Do not use rawhide if it is rotten; the smell, the slime, and the way it looks and feels are indicators to watch for. When cutting and stretching, it will break and look bad.

Storing - Salting a Cow Skin

Salting is a way of preserving a cow skin for years if it is done right. No more than one year is best. (I would not keep the skin salted in the summertime.) Open the cow skin flat with the hair side facing the ground. Then, using big salt grains, spread the salt so that it is pretty well covered. Salt is not expensive, so really be generous with it. Fold the skin onto the skin side, then the hair-on-hair and so on until you have a square looking pile of skin. Now tie it up with string like a package. Storing skins this way makes them easier to move around. Try to place the salted skin in a dry place at a slight angle so that the juices can run out away from the skin. An old bathtub with a metal cover works well. Make the tub so it can drain and animals cannot eat or spoil it. For the best result, do not keep it past the spring or warm weather.

When ready to use the cow skin, wash it to remove the salt before you start the process. Place the salted skin in a container of water for a day to get the salt and dirt out of the skin. Move the skin around in the water to help the process. Salted skins are a bit harder to take care of, so I would recommend that you use fresh skins if possible. Also, not having to salt the skin and remove the salt will save time.

Processing Skin - Needed Equipment

Fleshing a cow skin can be a very slow process, but it has to be done. Tools needed: a square edge drawknife, a sharp drawknife, a utility knife, a pulley and rope, three or four 50-gallon plastic barrels, cold hardwood ashes, hydrated lime, a standing tree to hold the pulley and a J hook to move the skin up and down from one barrel to another barrel, a sander for the beam, a plastic apron, a big knife to cuts scraps, a sharpening stone, plastic pail for waste, a rain jacket, tall rubber boots, a hat, safety goggles, rubber gloves with grips on them, rags to wipe off your knife, access to water, a block-and-tackle on a bench to hang up the skin. This will make it easier to split the skin in half if it is too big, a stirring stick and a short rope about 6-foot for holding the skin from the center of the neck. One end of the rope should be left outside of the barrel and easy to find when lifting the skin. When most of the water has run off the skin, cut the skin in half while still hanging. Then place it on the fleshing beam to remove the hair first.

When using the fleshing knife, keep safety in mind because it can cut. I took a two handed drawknife and straightened the handles with a torch and put on a slide stop block to stop my gloved hands from sliding onto the blade. I then bent it with the heat from a torch to round the blade a bit. Use the plastic apron, high rubber boots, safety goggles, and rubber gloves, to limit contact of solutions with your skin and to keep yourself dry and clean.

The fleshing beam can be made easily by taking a yellow birch log six feet long and splitting it in half. Remove the bark, drill two holes at a slight angle underneath, and place two peg legs into the holes toward the upward end of the beam. The beam, half a log, is placed at an angle of about 40 to 55 degrees. Different legs for different heights will help better position the skin for working. Take the bark off of half of the log, sanding the rough spots. A fleshing beam can also be purchased commercially. At times, sand or rub the fleshing beam to get the gashes out as they are made; I have made some accidental cuts on the beam at times. I always take a shower right after and wash my hands often!

Set-up

Preparing the rawhide is one of the major steps. (In the old days, the hide would be nailed to walls and allowed to dry. Then it would be dried hard. A sharp, slightly rounded tool would be used to scratch the hair off. This process could take days, since only about a quarter of an inch could be scraped at a time in short strokes.) The fall time or on a cool spring day before the bugs come out is a good time to remove the hair and flesh off the skin. One a day can be done for a few days. Working outside is best because it can smell a bit. After some time, you will not even smell it. That is why the skin has to be done right away. Wind can also help with the smell. Select a place where good footing is guaranteed. Make sure your fleshing beam cannot move. Secure it to a piece of plywood to be sure. Because the process of removing hair and flesh from skins requires a number of sharp tools, it is very important to create and maintain a clean and safe workspace. Always have sure

footing when moving the skins. Never be in a hurry to do anything; the extra time is worth your safety. Pay attention to what you are doing and try to complete the process before stopping because it is hard to start and stop.

Processing the Hide

The fresh hide is placed in cold water to make sure it stays wet and clean. The hide must be completely wet to process in a solution of hydrated lime and hardwood ashes. When applying hydrated lime, watch for the dust. Use a mask. In a plastic 55 gallon barrel over half full of water, you add three gallons of hydrated lime and three gallons of hardwood ashes. Stir well before putting the hide in it. (The solution requires one pint of lime and one pint of ash for each gallon of water.) Mix enough solution so the barrel will be more than half full depending on the size of the hide. Since you have to stir the hide with a wooden paddle four times per day for the solution to work well. It will be easier with more than enough solution. Don't make it strong enough to burn the skin.

Before placing the hide in the solution, cut a short slit at the center of the neck one inch in. Use that slit to lift the hide out of the solution. In the slit, tie a six foot light rope to help find where the slit is when the hide is in the solution. Keep the rope end outside the barrel. Stir the hide and solution to make sure every part of the hide is being treated. Cover the barrels so nothing can fall in.

If the weather is warm, the solution will work faster. After two days, start checking if the hair is coming off when it is stirred. With rubber gloves, pull the hair here and there to see if it will come off easily. If the weather is cool, it will take longer for the solution to work. The solution can be made stronger if needed. Use a set of block-and-tackle if the hide is heavy to move it up and stir it back down. With your gloves, take a pinch to see how loose it is. On the third day, start checking on the back of the neck towards the shoulders where the hairs are harder to loosen. It is best to try several different places on the skin. This hair test gives an accurate picture of the progress of the process. As soon as the hairs start slipping out easily, it is time to take it out of the solution. If it is not ready, drop it back into the barrel and wait another day. It can take from three to seven days for the solution to do its work. Again, please be safe in all you do, have a first aid kit available at all times and water to flush your eyes or wash your skin.

Once the hair slips off easy with your fingers, the hide is ready to be de-haired. Since the thickness of the skin is not the same everywhere, split the hide crosswise while it is hanging, about half way behind the shoulders, to keep the thicker backend together. The front end tends to be thinner and more elastic. Working on only half of the hide is easier. We have adjustable racks that one man can handle to stretch these two pieces to dry. Let the skin drip, overnight if needed, before putting it on the stretcher.

Removing Hair

The cowhides need to have all the hair removed first. Placing the skin on a fleshing beam, we use a straight handle drawknife with a rounded metal blade, using the square back edge of the blade to help remove the hair from the skin. The drawknife edge should be dull for removing hair. When removing the flesh and fat, something under the skin like hair, might make your blade dig into the skin. It does not matter with the hair side because the duller square edge is being used, and it will not cut the skin. I like to remove the hair in the center and then remove the rest clockwise until it is all done.

Push down on the hair with the square edge of the drawknife moving downward. Remove the hair as the lifted edge is pulled back, lightly rubbing the hair off. The hair, stuck on the square edge should be removed. Rub with gloves in some of the deep spots that

103

the drawknife cannot reach to remove all the hair. A flat scraper can help at times and can help remove hair. Also, there other tools can be tried. Take your time with this process; the more hair removed at this point, the less that will have to be removed just before weaving the snowshoes.

Jordan Labbe

Fleshing the Hide on the Beam

Once the hairs are removed, turn the hide over on the beam. The sharp edge of the drawknife, 13 inches or longer with a curved metal blade, is used for fleshing. It has handles on each side that are about 6 inches long. With this sharp flesher, we remove the tissue, flesh, and fat, leaving only the skin needed for snowshoes. We try not to cut through the hide. We find that using short strokes with this flesher works better and is less likely to make cuts in the skin. A few sharp meat cutting knifes can also help remove and cut the

unwanted skin around the outer edges. A J hook with a handle can be used to help move the skin on the wooded fleshing beam. Make holes on the outside edges to help with this task.

Fleshing is very hard work for the first skin, but the more skins you do, the easier it is. A very sharp fleshing knife is the key. Keep the fleshing knife sharp and sharpen the whole shining part of the blade, not just the tip. A watered stone is best. Keep sharpening it. Be careful with the big drawknife. I like doing a small amount at a time, maybe 18 inch strips because it is an easy reach and the weight on the blade handles will help cut through all the fat and meat to the skin.

We first use the big sharp drawknife on the flesh side, then the backend, dull, smaller draw shaver to get it cleaned to the skin. The saw side of the big draw shaver can be used to remove some of the flesh and meat if it is stuck hard to the skin, but I hardly use it. Use the drawer shaver in a sawing motion to remove the flesh off the skin. There are many approaches for using the drawknife to remove flesh from the skin. Experiment and find a process that works. Having a partner to help with the cleanup of the skin makes the process go much faster.

The back of the skin end is harder to do because sometimes the flesh is really stuck on. Cut off all the bad spots and pieces that stick out a bit on the skin and around the neck. Trimming around the neck, where the hide is too thick to work, will help save money and time. Do not process skin that can not be used. Again, ensure fleshing beam is secure. Keep your back straight when fleshing and take breaks as needed. Wear high boots, an apron, and plastic gloves. Remember, the area around the skin will be slippery and wet; take time and be careful when handling sharp tools.

The skin at this time is thick and swollen because the solution has caused the pores to open. The skin is then washed in cold water and placed in a solution of lactic acid (two ounces of lactic acid for every ten gallons of water) for twenty-four hours to prevent the skin from being damaged. The skin should be stirred in this solution at least four times in the 24 hours. Apple cider vinegar can be used if lactic acid is not available. It neutralizes the action. The skin is then washed in about 70 degree water. It is hung up to drain to make it lighter. This is done before placing on a square rack to dry. If you wanted to make leather, this would be the right time, since the pores are still open. A slight smell is okay. If it is too smelly and slimy, then it is probably rotten and not good to use.

Preparing your own skins is hard, somewhat smelly, and slippery work, but with a little practice, you'll soon be able to handle several skins in a day. Preparing your own skins will save you money, and working with materials you helped prepare is an important part of being a traditional snowshoe maker.

Stretching

Working on a large table or while still hanging makes cutting the skin in half easier than cutting it on the ground. The skin now can be preserved by stretching it on an adjustable rack made into a square with four pieces of square peace of spruce wood, 2 inches by 3 inches width and at least 5½ feet width by 8½ feet length, until it is dry. Poles can also be made into a square frame big enough to fit the half hide.

The stretcher is made adjustable by drilling holes in the wood overlap a little bigger than the corner bolts. On the inside of the rack, fence staples are placed on the frame. The holes should be six inches apart all around on the three inch side of the frame so when the piece of skin is placed inside of the rack on top of a table, it can be adjusted allowing for some stretch. As it dries, opening some slits may be needed to give some slack on the frame so it does not twist as much. (The frame can also be used to dry and stretch leather.)

We make our S-hooks to hold the skin with two and half inch nails (6-penny nails). The use of regular nails are best because the rust holds the skin better. We make the hooks by using two five inch spikes in a vise with the points sticking up above the vise about one inch. They are just far enough apart to pass a two and half inch nail in between them. With a large pair of pliers, we take a nail by the pointed end and place the head of the nail in between the spike ends and go around one of the ends creating a loop. Lift the loop and place it on the far point of the spike and turn the nail around the second end of the spike finishing the hook.

Use four 1/8 inch braided rope to thread through the staples on the rack on each side of the wood of the rack. Leave about 3 feet of extra braided rope. Pliers can then be used to close in the end of the S-hook between the staples so that it does not come off the rope. The hooks that hold the hide can slide on the rope around the frame to tighten the skin. Place the S-hook point downwards to hold the skin. Place an extra hook at the end of the two fence staples. Use that last hook to help hold the rope tight. Just run the hook back and hold on one of the ropes that are holding the skin.

Start (1) on the center of the straight cut side of the skin and on the eight and a half foot (estimate) side of the rack. Run a strong, nylon braided line from the center fence staple, working through the skin hooks and fence staples toward the right (2). Tie off the slack end from the last staple on an extra hook on the skin or on an extra staple. Do the same moving left from the straight

edge (3) to the end of the pole (4). Continue with the staple and hook combination on the opposite side (5) starting from one end ending on the other. Repeat on the last two sides (6 and 7). Once the skin is hooked in the rack, it is easy to tighten or loosen. Your hooks should point in the same direction. This method is efficient, centering the skin on the rack and limiting the waste.

A pointed knife is best to make the slot in the skin edges. Keep this knife sharp. The slot that you will make should only be a bit bigger than the nail. Make your slots about ⅛ inch from the edge of the skin so that you do not waste the rawhide.

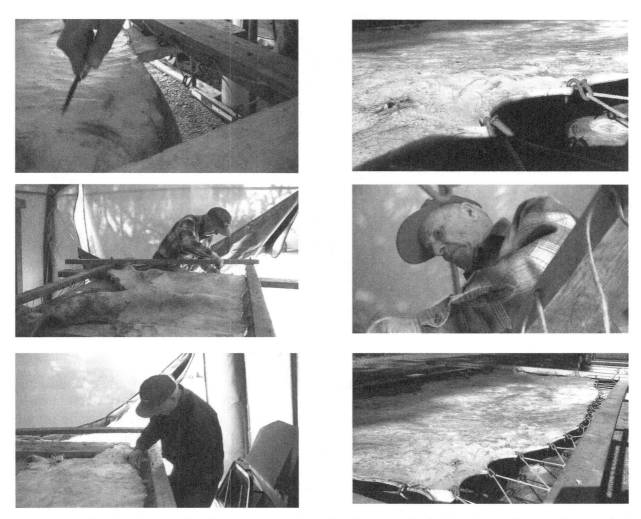

It will take from a few days to a week to dry the stretched skin depending on heat and air humidity. Do not put in direct sunlight or where it is too hot. A fan may also be used to speed up the drying process of the skin. You will want to give the skin some slack as it is tightening. Even if the skin is not completely dry, you still may take it off the stretcher as long as it is fairly stiff. It will finish drying in time.

Once dried, the skin can be taken off the stretcher, rolled, and tied. It can be used whenever it is needed. Make sure you store it in a dry place where animals cannot get to it. Cut the skin crosswise in half to keep the thicker back together and the thinner shoulder and thicker neck section together. This is only done when a whole skin is ready to cut up. The thicker hide is used for snowshoes made for heavier people or for wrapping the ends. Cut it into strips for weaving any time by soaking the rolled skin in a barrel of water until you can find the soft and thin sections. This can be found on the belly sections of the skin. The underside belly of the animal softens first because it is thinner. Remove and save these pieces to cut later for weaving the ends of the snowshoes. With a knife, separate the thinner skin to

be used for the ends of the snowshoes where less pressure is applied. The thicker section is used for the centers where the weight is carried. In both cases, you cut around the pieces.

Cutting

The French word for cut rawhide strips is 'babiche'. A good piece of rawhide is needed to give the snowshoe strength and a better appearance. If there is a defect, it can be cut off or marked to later remove while cutting. Do not try to cut too big a piece of rawhide because it will take a longer time to cut, and it will be more difficult to maneuver. It will also have more stretchy parts throughout the piece that needs to be considered and cut out. Remove the outer skin holes first. Cut along the outer edge going around the whole piece, cutting corners as they become sharp corners. Thin pieces of rawhide should be used right after it is cut. If not, freeze in the snow in a plastic bag or dry it until needed. If it is frozen, put it in water for about an hour or so, keeping an eye on it for use when it is ready. Just let it thaw out a bit at a time, while checking it periodically. Dried rawhide can be put in water to soak over night. The thickness of the rawhide is an important factor for deciding how long to let it soak. Repeated thawing helps determine needed time for different widths and sizes.

Rawhide Cutting Table w/Heavy Wheel: When cutting, we clamp a five inch long, one and three quarter inch block of wood with a half inch slot at one end with a slit made, with a hack saw, to insert a utility blade. We made marks on the block next to the blade to show how wide we are cutting. Once we have cut two or three feet of rawhide by hand, we anchor the end to a shaft that has a heavy three foot diameter wheel that pulls the raw hide when it turns. The weight of the wheel creates a steady tension that cuts smoothly as the wheel is turned. With the right hand, we turn the wheel and with the left hand, we guide the width of the rawhide on a table in a continual circle. We can start and stop instantly. The cutting with this wheel also helps stretching and even narrowing the width when cutting. The utility knife is a sharp tool with an exposed blade that can be used to cut the square corners off the pieces and to help trim off the bad spots. Once, every three or four skins, or when the pulling gets too hard, change blades in your cutter.

Small Rawhide Cutting Tool (Rawhide Sizing Holes w/3 Hole Craft Blade): When cutting the thin smaller rawhide for the ends of the snowshoes, you drill a hole the same size you will have to pass through on the snowshoes, right on the edge of a block of maple, clamped to the table. Screw in a small blade that will form a part of the hole that the rawhide will pass through. Cut a narrow strip a few inches long using the utility knife, then use pliers to pull it through the hole with the blade until you can reach the shaft with the wheel. The rawhide you are

using can have different thickness and stretchiness, so by forcing it through the blade, you are stretching it, sizing it, and cutting it at the same time. This rawhide is ready to be used.

After you have finish cutting the hide into wide or thin webbing, you roll it loosely so it can dry to be used whenever needed. Cut the skin into strips for weaving any time by soaking the rolled hide in a barrel of water until the heaviest part of the skin has softened, making it easier to find the thinner sections that are usually on the belly. The thicker and stronger part of the skin will be cut three eight to half inch wide by cutting around the piece.

It will be easier to cut the thicker and stronger part into strips for weaving the center parts of the snowshoe, if the skin is somewhat still stiff. Depending on the thickness of the skin, cut the strip between 3/8 inch and $\frac{1}{4}$ inch wide, by cutting around the piece. Going around, keep rounding the sharp corners with a utility knife. The small thick pieces with all the bends can be used for wrapping top/back ends. Sharp turns are weaker. The long strip of rawhide can be rolled loosely on the rack or spools for faster rolling and removal. It will also be easier to dry when used later as needed. Date the skin with a pencil when it when finished. Place it in a dry place where it will be safe from animals and moisture.

When cutting the thicker hide for center weaving, cut ½ inch to ⅜ inch wide. At first do not try to cut a piece bigger than you can handle. Feel the thickness with your hands as you turn it while cutting. A round piece of rawhide is easier to handle and to cut, but you tend to have more waste. Odd shapes are fine. When you come to holes or cuts in the hide, cut them off just before you get there and keep going. Always have the flesh side of the hide upwards so it will be easier to see the cuts and defects as you come to them. The real thick rawhide is used for the biggest snowshoe centers. Use the thinner rawhide for the smaller snowshoe.

Fine Cutting for Ends

To cut strips for weaving the snowshoe ends, use the pieces of thin skins of different thickness and stretchiness. Use only about 18 inch by 18 inch pieces of thin rawhide at first and a skin with the same thickness throughout to make it easier. Soak the pieces of skin until fully soft, and then start by cutting a strip with a sharp knife. This strip will go through a hole the size of the holes on the ends of snowshoes with a small blade on one side of the hole that will cut the strip once the hole is full of stretched hide.

Keep the similar rawhides together. Do not leave rawhide wet or moist too long because it will smell and start to deteriorate. A cap full of tide detergent in five gallons of water can help reduce the smell of the rawhide before using it. You will soon find out how soft you like it when cutting the rawhide. Hold the skin upward with one hand while cutting on the piece as the other hand turns the wheel. The wheel is big and heavy, pulling the rawhide down

with a lot of power. If the skin is extra thin at places, it is no good for webbing the ends.

Once it has been passed through the sizing hole, keep checking every 20 inches or so, that it is the right size. You want the small rawhide to fit snug in the snowshoe frame holes. A tester can be made in a piece of wood with a hole and a V slot taken out of the wood. Place it in the V slot to see if it fits snug in the hole. Once the rawhide is dry for a few minutes it will shrink. Also, keep in mind that the hole on the frame is one size bigger. If the rawhide breaks after the hole, change the blade or cut a bit off the piece of rawhide at the hole. You may come across places that just break for unknown reasons. Do not be concerned with those pieces, just get rid of them. Twisting the rawhide while weaving makes the small rawhide stronger, like yarn, and makes it look better and more balanced on the snowshoe.

Caring for Rawhide

When rawhide is dry, it will keep for a long time. Rawhide can be wet and dry many times. When it is needed, let it soak in water. You can let it dry, and the process then starts all over again when you soak it over night. The thicker the rawhide, the longer you will need to keep it in the water to get it soft before using. As rawhide dries, it tightens to give it more strength. Cutting your own rawhide into strips is the best because you can control for quality.

Tips

1. When weaving the ends of the snowshoes, do not pull too tight because it will not look right once they are done. The rawhide tightens as it dries.

2. Do not weave dry rawhide. It is hard on the hands and will not stretch or twist very well. Wet the rawhide as needed so that it is workable.

3. Change the water often so that it does not go stale (smells). A bit of tide detergent will go a long way

4. Burning the hair off is a big mistake because the rawhide will lose its strength and you may not know it until the snowshoes are put under pressure. It burns the woven strands within the skin and makes it weaker.

5. The sizing hole should be checked for hair and skin; it should be kept clean. If this is not done, it will change the size of the rawhide.

6. Use the neck of the animal, the heavier rawhide, for making strips for wrapping, front, backs, and to repair old snowshoes because it is not very nice looking rawhide, but still works.

7. Put all your tools away once done and clean all your tools so rust does not get to it. A light oil rag helps on the metal tools. Also clean the mess. You do not need other things to happen or animal to get into this.

Glenn and Jordan Labbe

Robert Pelletier, Jr

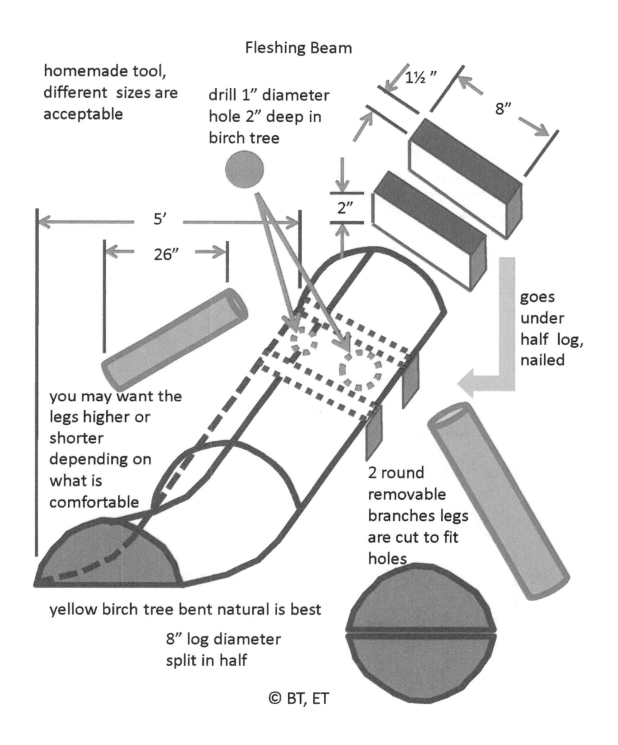

Fleshing Beam

homemade tool, different sizes are acceptable

drill 1" diameter hole 2" deep in birch tree

1½ "

8"

2"

5'

26"

goes under half log, nailed

you may want the legs higher or shorter depending on what is comfortable

2 round removable branches legs are cut to fit holes

yellow birch tree bent natural is best

8" log diameter split in half

© BT, ET

Center Rawhide Hardwood Cutting Tool
-see on page 3 of 3

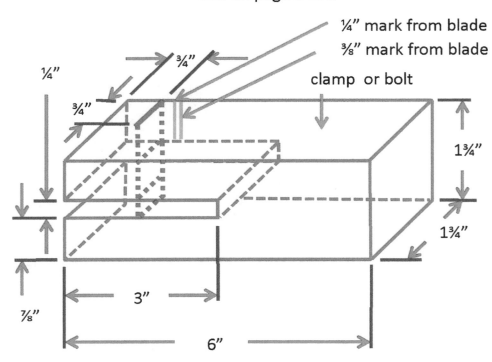

¼" mark from blade

⅜" mark from blade

clamp or bolt

¾"

¼"

¾"

1¾"

1¾"

3"

⅞"

6"

hacksaw cut for unity blade to be placed in tight and flush with wood

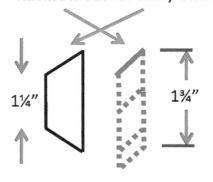

1¼"

1¾"

snap off extra
part of blade that
is extended
above wood

© BT, ET

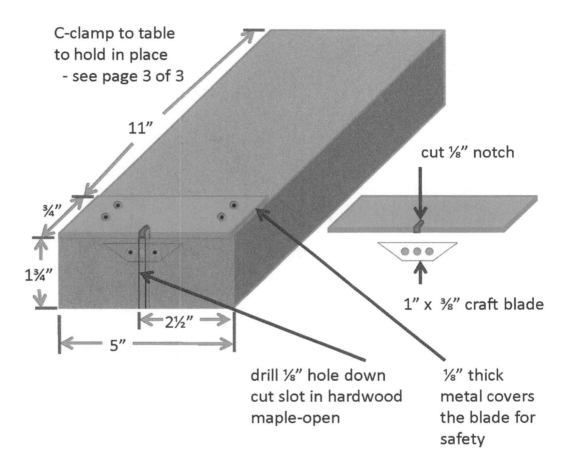

C-clamp to table
to hold in place
- see page 3 of 3

11"

¾"

1¾"

2½"

5"

cut ⅛" notch

1" x ⅜" craft blade

drill ⅛" hole down
cut slot in hardwood
maple-open

⅛" thick
metal covers
the blade for
safety

- just a hole in blade, no screw
- Pre drill hole and small screws

© BT, ET

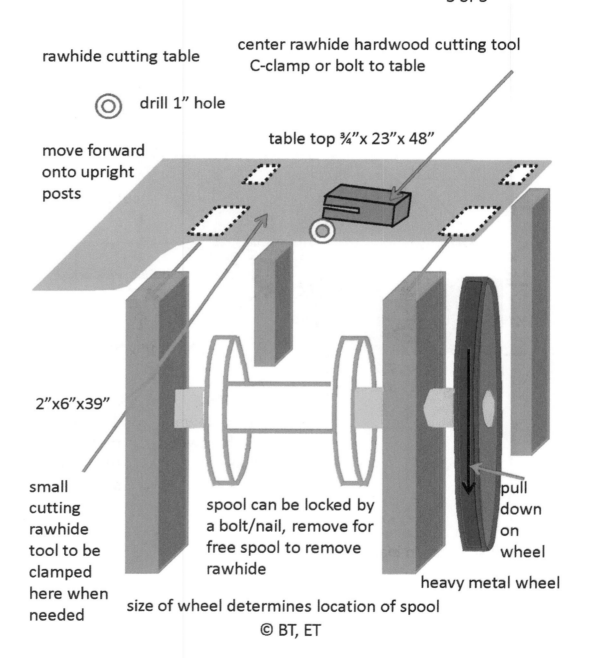

rawhide cutting table

center rawhide hardwood cutting tool
C-clamp or bolt to table

drill 1" hole

table top ¾"x 23"x 48"

move forward
onto upright
posts

2"x6"x39"

small
cutting
rawhide
tool to be
clamped
here when
needed

spool can be locked by
a bolt/nail, remove for
free spool to remove
rawhide

pull
down
on
wheel

heavy metal wheel

size of wheel determines location of spool
© BT, ET

Notes:

Chapter 7 - Weaving

Maddie Theriault

The weaving can be tricky until you learn the different techniques. You need to know how soft the rawhide should be and when to add water to keep it at the right pliability when weaving. Try to keep it clean from dirt of other materials. Cut enough of the same part or piece so the rawhide looks alike. Take out only what is needed as it will soil if left out. A little tide laundry detergent will help with the smell and slime. If it gets wet too long, it will be bad when it dries or freezes and thaws again. Clean the rawhide anytime there is fat or meat left on the strips by cutting it off or scraping it with the knife before weaving. Avoid narrower rawhide because it breaks easily while weaving and wears out quickly when snowshoes are used a lot.

Preparing Rawhide for the Centers

Before weaving, soak the rawhide in water for 24 hours. Then, pre-stretch it by wrapping it around a 16 inch diameter, 15 inch length piece of a wooden log, preferably hardwood, that has been split in half (stretcher block). This is used for stretching the wide rawhide before using it for the center of the snowshoe. In the split, we have cut out a space where we can insert a 2-ton hydraulic jack in the log's center to stretch the rawhide. Two square 6 x 8 inch, ¾ inch thick plywood pieces are used to cover the holes in the center of both ends. Spikes are placed in the four corner holes to attach it to the log ends. There is a center hole for a metal round bar to pass between the two pieces of the log. The metal bar is used to place the log on a stand to allow it to turn as you wrap the rawhide. Once all is in place with the plywood spikes on each side, the stand will have two upright hardwood sides with a half-rounded hole that holds this pipe.

Step 1: Put the stretching block together: two halves of log, square, and pipe.
Step 2: Put the stretching block pipe on the holder.
Step 3: Nail (small nail) end of rawhide on the right hand side of the stretching block.
Step 4: Holding rawhide flat, hair up, wrap the wide wet rawhide to cover the log. You can put two layers.
Step 5: Nail second end where it finishes.
Step 6: Take pipe off rack and put on platform.
Step 7: Remove pipe and two squares at the ends.
Step 8: Place 2-ton jack upright within the center of the stretching block.
Step 9: Start jacking slowly as you hammer between the block separation to evenly stretch the rawhide for about an inch.
Step 10: Wait a few minutes.
Step 11: Do another inch.
Step 12: Put in wooded wedges between split log to hold in place.
Step 13: Remove the jack.
Step 14: Wait 30 minutes on the stretching block.

Step 15: Place the stretching block on one end.

Step 16: Take out last placed nail and unravel rawhide placing it in a bucket as you take it off the log.

Step 17: Take off first placed nail.

  If not all of it is use, keep it frozen or in a cold place until it is needed. The cut rawhide should be soaked over night.

Weaving Centers

  We find it easier to weave the centers first, since passing the rawhide through the small ends of the frame is faster. The small holes left by the top and bottom weaving would make weaving the center more difficult because it is easier to handle the rawhide by the handful. Use a pencil to mark on the side of the frame where the strong half-inch rawhide will cross over from side-to-side. Large Cross Country/Large Green Mountain--The first mark is at four inches from the front crosspiece on both sides. The second mark is two inches from the first mark and the next four marks are at 1¾ inch intervals. Other types may have slight variations. The snowshoe frames are now ready for the three-way weave with rawhide. The same pattern is used for center weaving, but the spacing will be different.

  The center can be woven on a flat chair with an opening in the back to pass the end of the snowshoe frame through. A 2 x 4 inch block under the front legs of the chair will tilt the frame upwards and help position the snowshoes. A cushion on the seat covering the snowshoe frame will help protect the frame and will be more comfortable. It will also keep you off the wet rawhide. Each snowshoe will be woven identically, since there is no left or right snowshoe.

  About 45 feet of rawhide is what is needed for the center on one snowshoe and should be all in one piece. This is best so that there are no knots on the sides. Never put knots in the middle

of the snowshoe because it does not look good, and

it will wear as it takes a beating. Put a knot on the side if it is needed. Keep the rawhide tight and keep the flat scraped hair upwards on the center when weaving. This is the top of the snowshoe and you want it to look good.

The weaving needs to be strong and secure so when you are walking, there is a bounce when you lift your foot, similar to walking on a trampoline. To get a firm weave, a good rawhide is needed that has been pre-stretched and tied on wooded frames so that no matter how the snowshoes are used, the knots will not move. If the knots move, it means some slack happened somewhere, and some of the bounce is lost. If it is too tight at places, you will get a loose up-and-down weave with a straight strand.

To make sure the rawhide is tight, weave from knot to knot loosely. Then go back to the last tight knot, and with two hands, tighten each small part until the last knot is tied. After some practice, this will be able to done automatically. Stop often and look at the lines of rawhide to make sure they are over and under the same way. The heart, the spot where the weaving over and under starts in the center, tells where weaving will finish. Follow the patterns at the end of the chapter for the four types of snowshoes. For very wide or bigger snowshoes (patterns not included): Depending on the size of snowshoes or how many times you want to go around with the rawhide, add more cross weaves before starting the weaving in the middle.

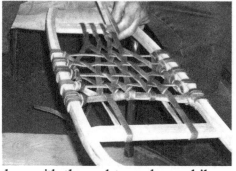

Before putting on any of the rawhide, double-check it. If there is a stretchy part, that piece will not be good to use. The rawhide should all be about the same width. Sit on the snowshoe with the end turned up while weaving the frames. This allows the top of the snowshoe to be seen. While weaving the middle, remember to keep the hide grain side up and that all the knots are the same.

While weaving, stop often to look at your work. Remember that what is done on one side, has to be done on the other side, to keep the weaving even. Once you have passed the rawhide over the center of the back crosspiece, you will be able to see better if you are weaving correctly, by comparing it with adjacent strips going the same way. The over and under pattern can be easily confused before you actually start doing the weaving.

Make sure to leave room for

the leather bindings on the side of the toe hole. The reason for large holes and wide leather is that the buckles are about ¾ inch. The placement of the bindings is with the buckles on the outside of your foot for easier removal. Also the bindings will not hit each other. This will determine which foot is correct, left or right. A piece of wood, the shape of a wedge, can be used between the rawhide sides to enlarge the binding holes while they are drying.

The wrapping of the main strand is done before the center dries too hard (about 15 feet of rawhide). The main strand wrapping is not only to protect the main strand, but to hold the main strand in place and to keep the center weaving from moving down. It is easily replaceable if it wears out. Use a little wider and thicker rawhide. After about one hour of weaving the center on the frame, hammer the main strand kind of flat where you place your shoe, so there is no bump when walking. Also, put the wrapping tight and hammer lightly again just to make sure it is flat before it dries.

Optional: Wrapping the front will help protect the front of your snowshoes in rough places, while you are using them. Fifteen feet of rawhide for the front end wrapping of the snowshoe webbing may be needed. Use the stretchy pieces of rawhide.

Weaving Top (front) / Bottom (back) Section

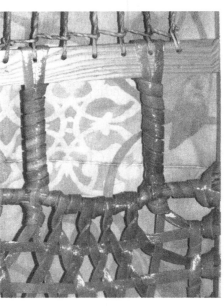

Keep the design on paper or a wooden frame sample so you can always go back to check on how you did it. You may design your own pattern 3-way (triangle) weave, if you think it is

easier. There are reasons for the three-way weave. It holds everything together better and keeps the weaving strong. The weaving rawhide will move less if it is done correctly. The bigger holes within the weaving allow the snow, of all types, to just go through so you are not carrying extra weigh. If it is a big snowshoe, you may have to go across more often but it is basically the same waving pattern.

Fresh cut thin rawhide is used for the frame ends. (Stored rawhide can also be used.) Rawhide has fine yarn-like hairs in the middle, which are stronger once twisted. Twisting the rawhide while weaving will give the rawhide a more balanced look. It is a bit slow at first, but it is what you want for your snowshoes to be the best you can make. Just remember to twist it all the way through.

Weaving the pattern with one piece of rawhide is sometimes tricky because the extra rawhide can get in the way. If you make a knot to connect pieces, you should put it along the edge of the frame, so they will not show up as much and the weaving will look smooth. To make the knot, you cut a slit on one end of two pieces. Pass one slit end through the other slit. Pass the opposite end of the rawhide, the piece with the filled slit, through the other slit, pulling the rawhide completely through the hole. This should make a flat knot. You may have to clamp it as it dries to make it flatter.

My father and I weave the ends on the "hop-on-pop" chair, a chair specially designed to hold the frame still while weaving the top and bottom of the snowshoe in front of you. (The same chair as the center weaving can also be used.)

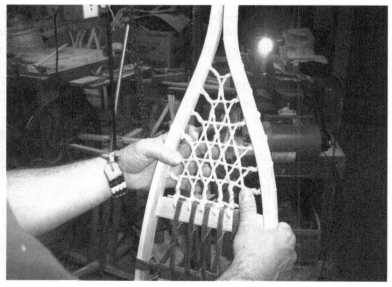

Finishing the Snowshoe

Using a screwdriver to straighten the finished center, slide it up and then back down to help keep the rawhide flat and spaced. Adjust the rawhide so that it is even and straight. It is easier to move when still a little wet. With a utility knife, get rid of any small pieces that may stick out on the rawhide. Place the snowshoes back-to-back to ensure that both shoes look alike.

Make sure the rawhide is well dried before varnishing the snowshoes. Sand the snowshoe lightly before varnishing, and a little more after the first coat. Hang the snowshoes in a vented area to dry. Brush off varnish drips as the snowshoes hang. Dry each coat completely. It usually takes two coats, the second being high-gloss.

Bindings

Leather hinged bindings (H-bindings) keep the foot secure and allow the snowshoer to remove the shoe easily. You do not want your foot to twist, if you fall, or your foot to get caught. Leather will give.

Center Rawhide Stretcher

- ● ¼" hole
- 8 -5" spikes
- ◎ ¾" hole

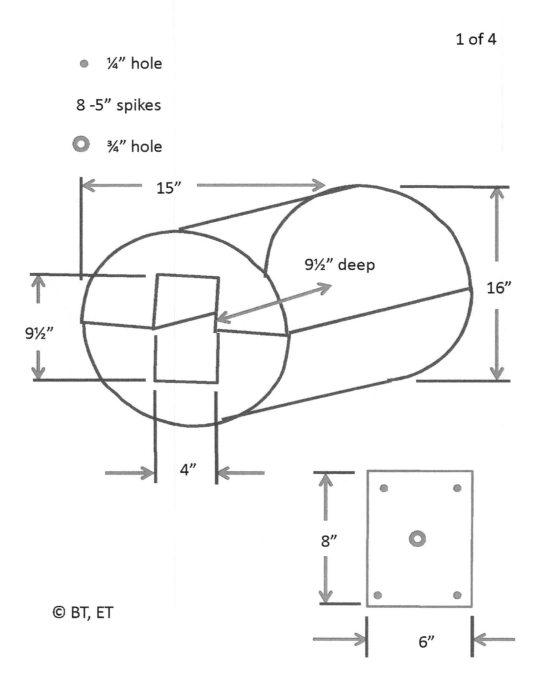

15"

9½" deep

9½"

16"

4"

8"

6"

© BT, ET

Center Rawhide Stretcher

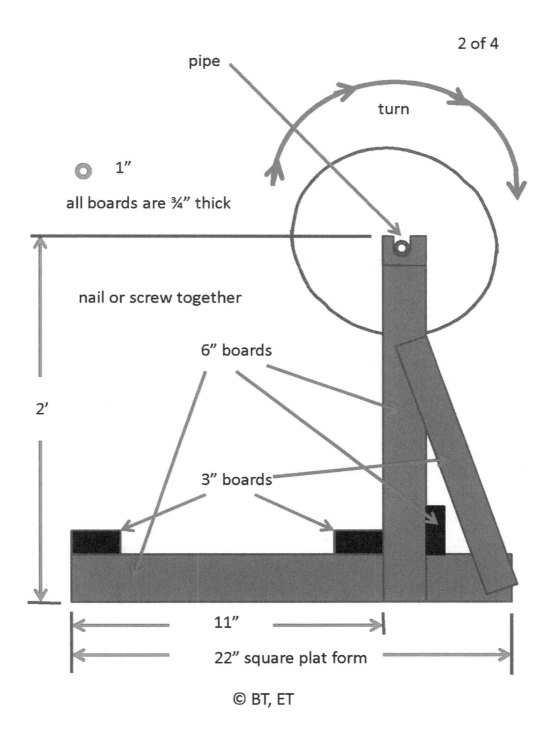

pipe

turn

1"

all boards are ¾" thick

nail or screw together

6" boards

3" boards

2'

11"

22" square plat form

© BT, ET

Center Rawhide Stretcher Round Log Block

3 of 4

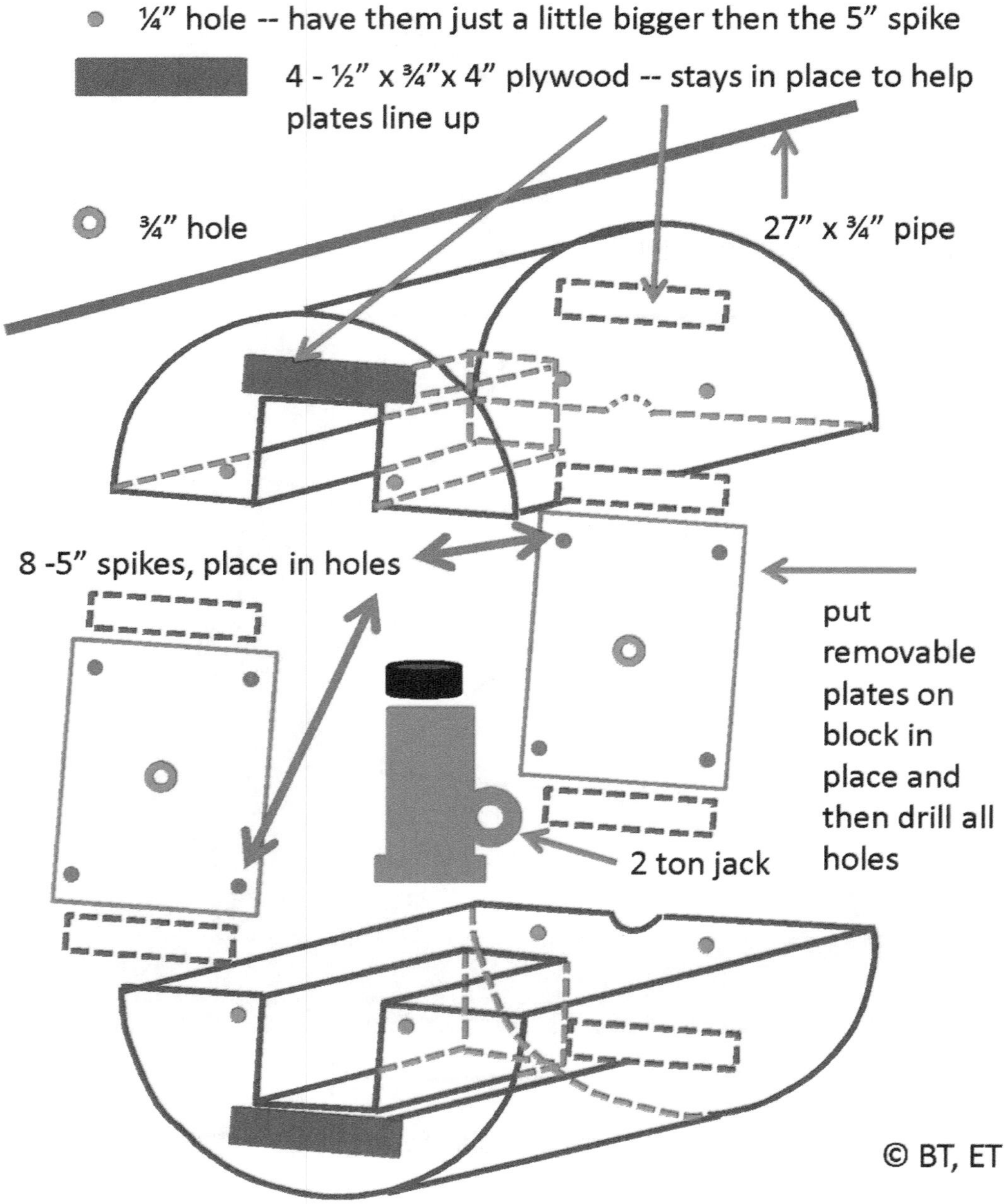
¼" hole -- have them just a little bigger then the 5" spike
4 - ½" x ¾"x 4" plywood -- stays in place to help plates line up
¾" hole
27" x ¾" pipe
8 -5" spikes, place in holes
put removable plates on block in place and then drill all holes
2 ton jack
© BT, ET

Center Rawhide Stretcher Round Log Block

¼" hole- have them just a little bigger then the 5" spike

4 - ½" x ¾"x 4" plywood-stays in place to help plates line up

8 -5" spikes

27" x ¾" pipe

¾" hole

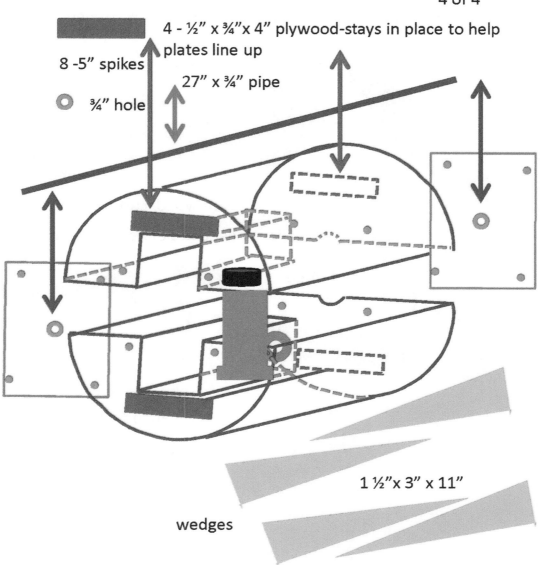

1 ½"x 3" x 11"

wedges

© BT, ET

Rawhide Splice

this works for any size strips of rawhide for 100 % strength

cut both ends of
rawhide on corner of
the wood

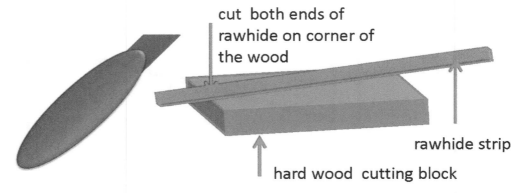

rawhide strip

hard wood cutting block

flatten rawhide with pliers if needed before cutting slot

then pull the other end three

2

1

pull end threw slot

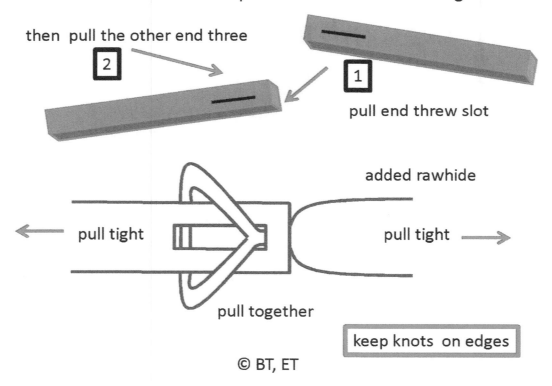

added rawhide

← pull tight

pull tight →

pull together

keep knots on edges

© BT, ET

130

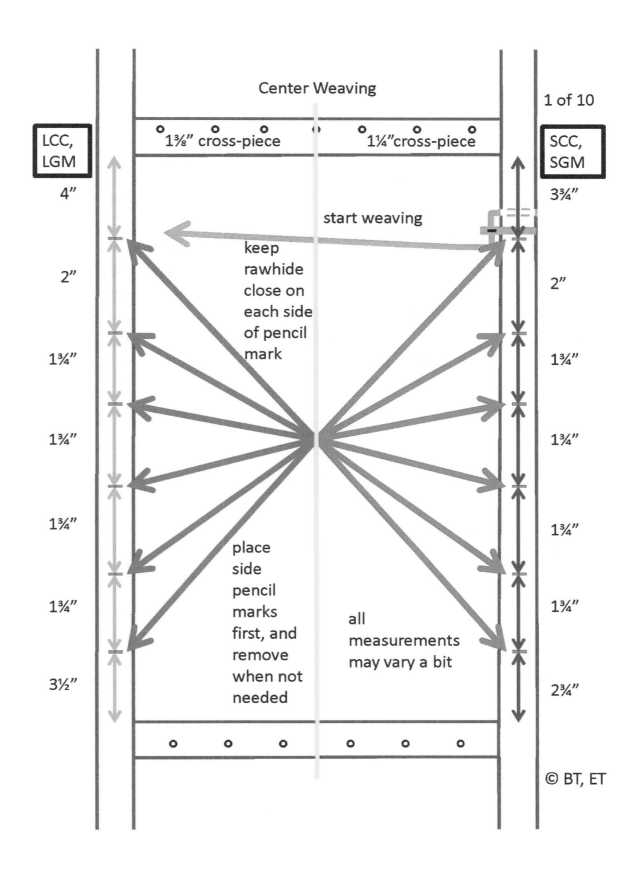

Center Weaving

LCC,
LGM

SCC,
SGM

1⅜" cross-piece   1¼"cross-piece

4"   3¾"

start weaving

keep
rawhide
close on
each side
of pencil
mark

2"   2"

1¾"   1¾"

1¾"   1¾"

1¾"   1¾"

place
side
pencil
marks
first, and
remove
when not
needed

all
measurements
may vary a bit

1¾"   1¾"

3½"   2¾"

© BT, ET

131

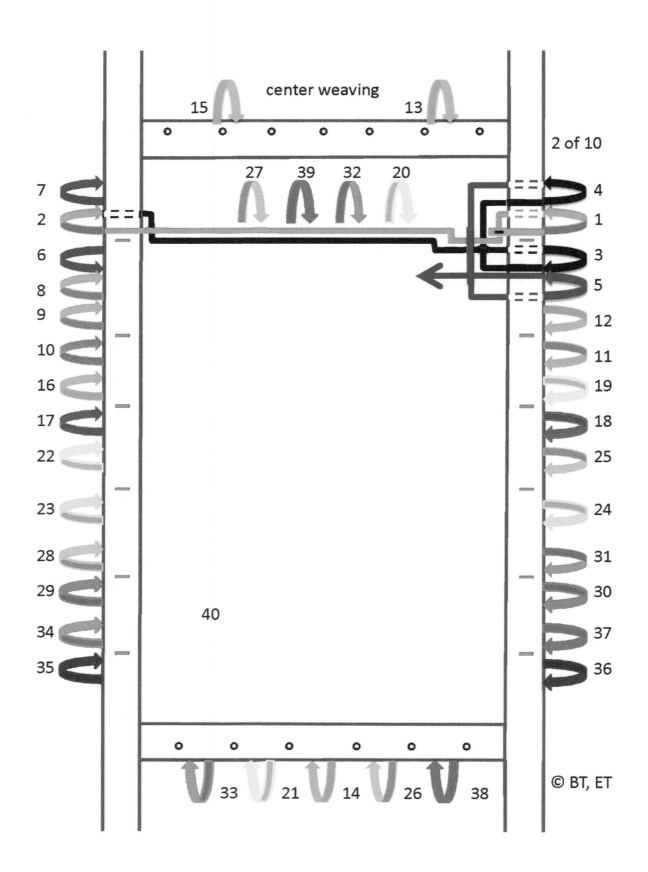

© BT, ET

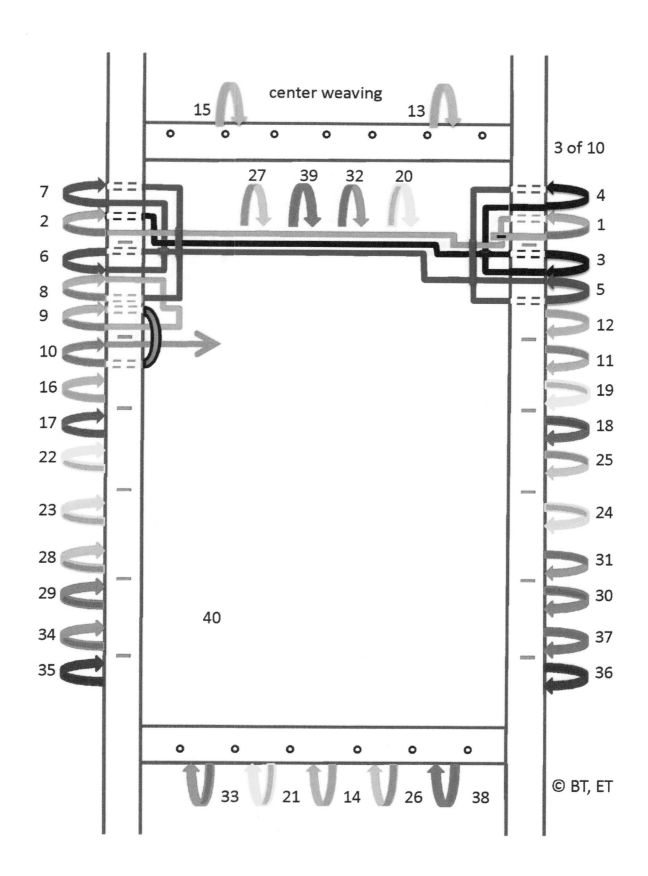

© BT, ET

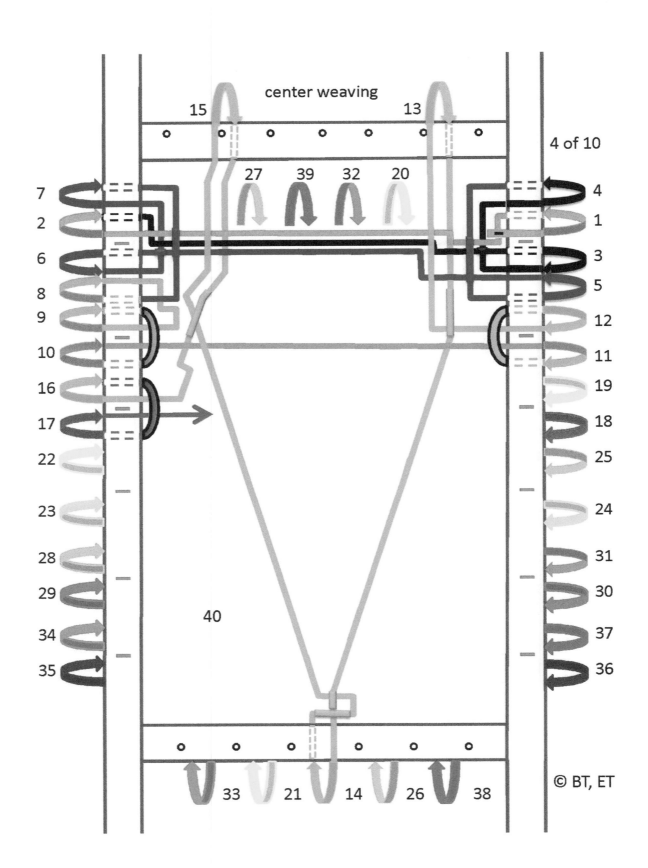

© BT, ET

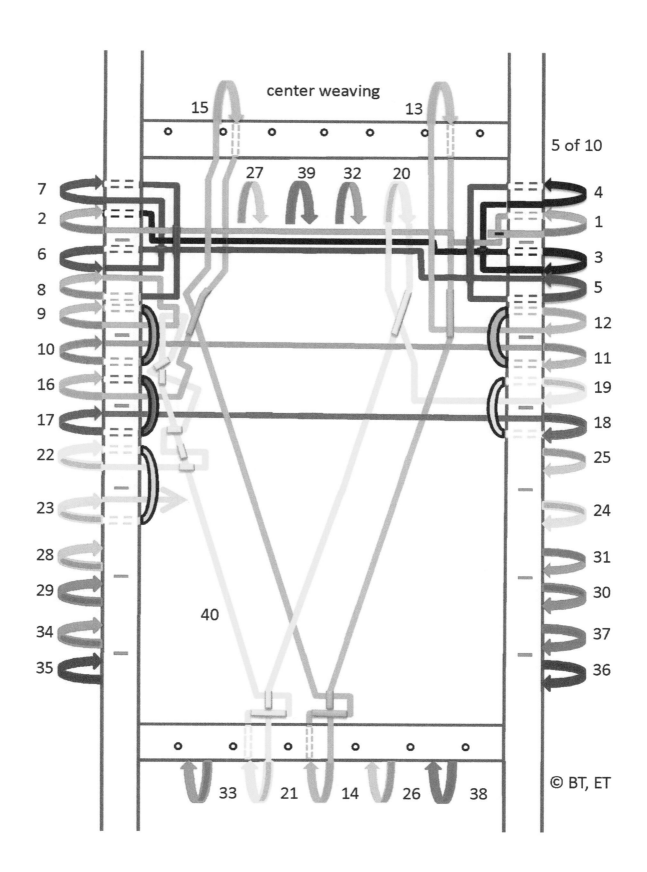

center weaving

© BT, ET

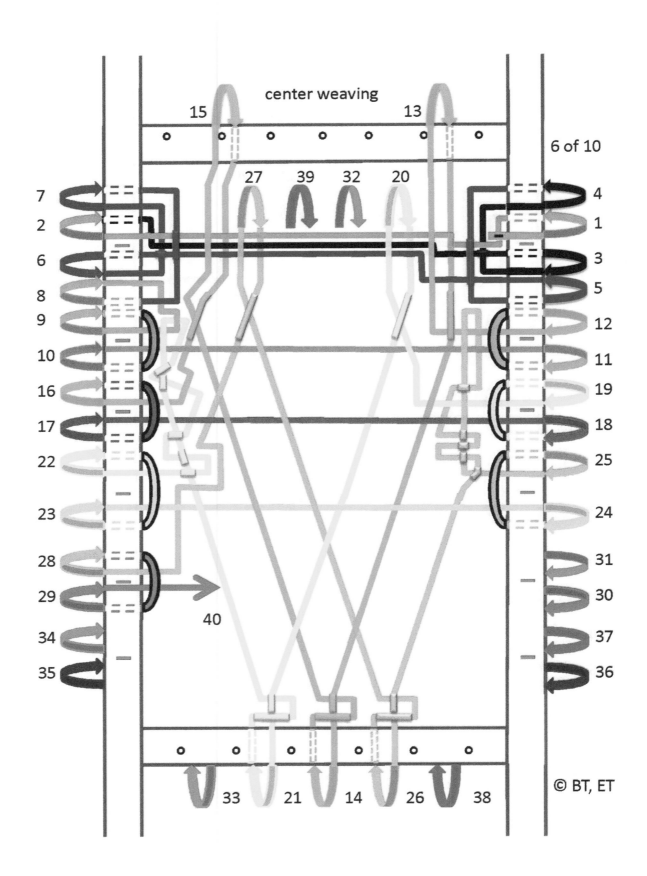

© BT, ET

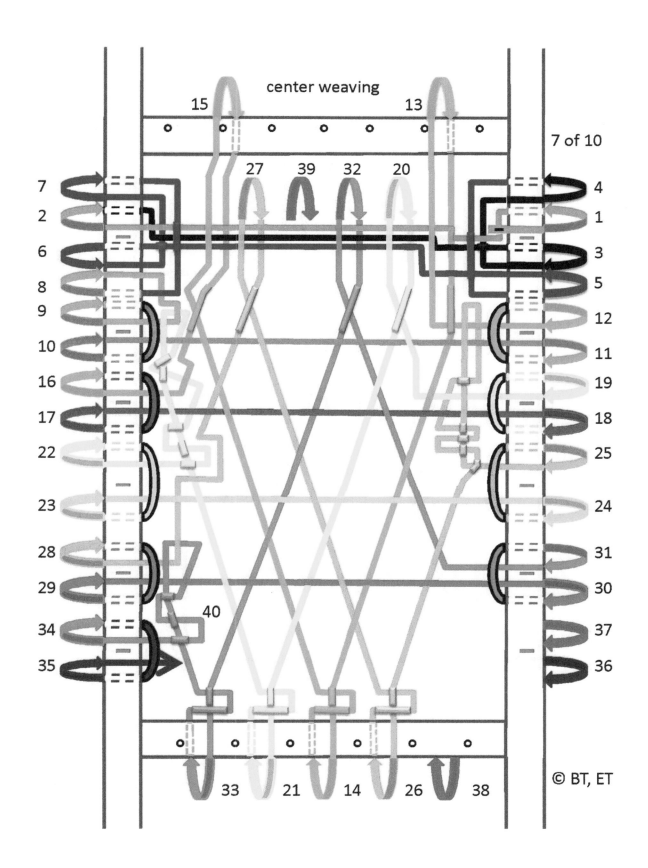

center weaving

© BT, ET

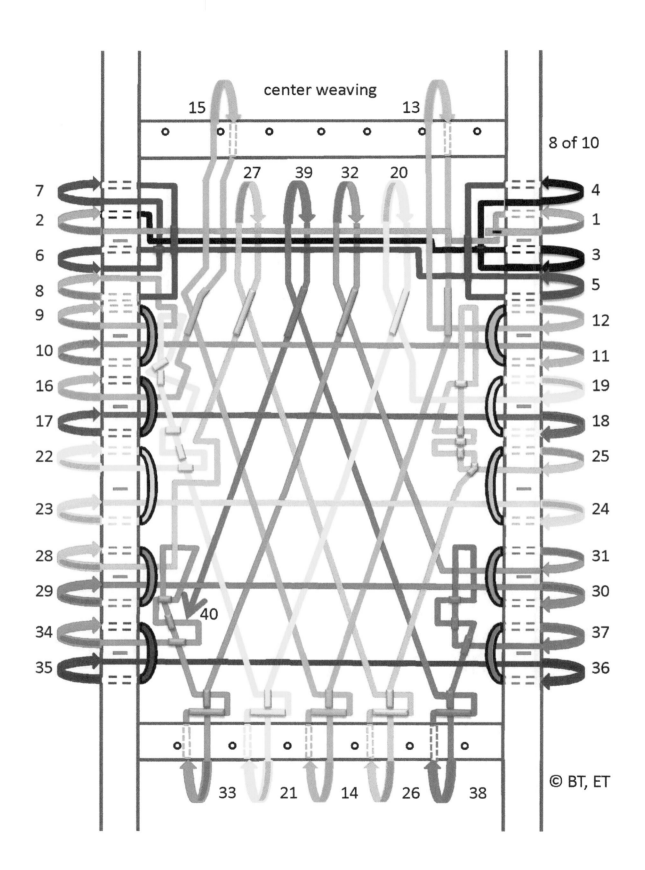

center weaving

15   13

27   39   32   20

7   4
2   1
6   3
8   5
9   12
10   11
16   19
17   18
22   25
23   24
28   31
29   30
34   37
35   36

40

33   21   14   26   38

© BT, ET

138

Center End Knot

Over-hand knot

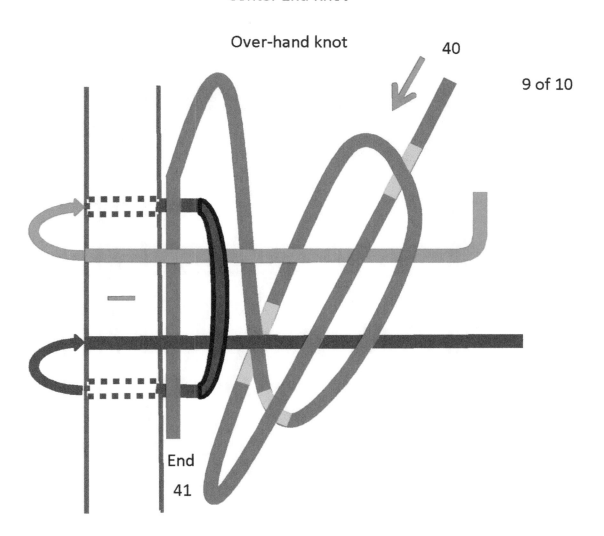

End

41

© BT, ET

Main strand wrapping

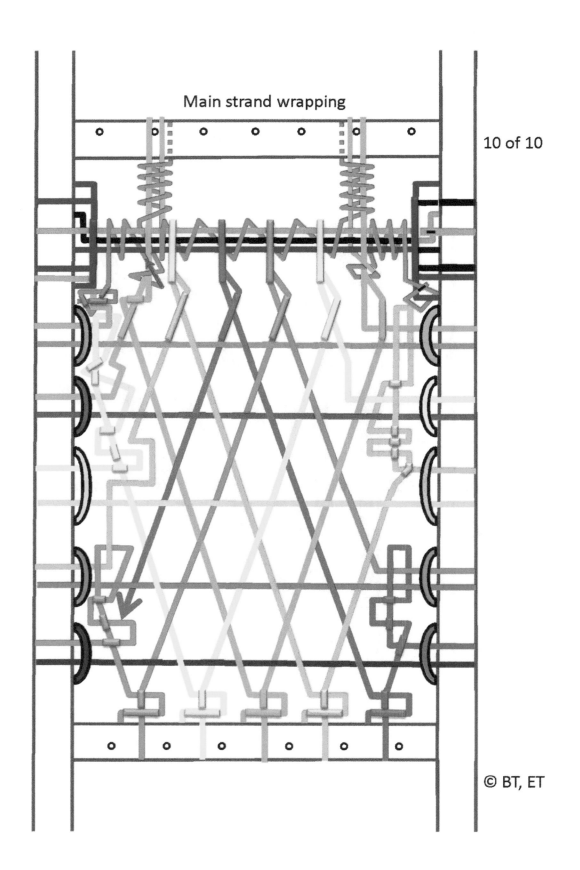

© BT, ET

Pom-Pom Maker

3"x 1"x 1" wood, yarn, 2-8 penny nails

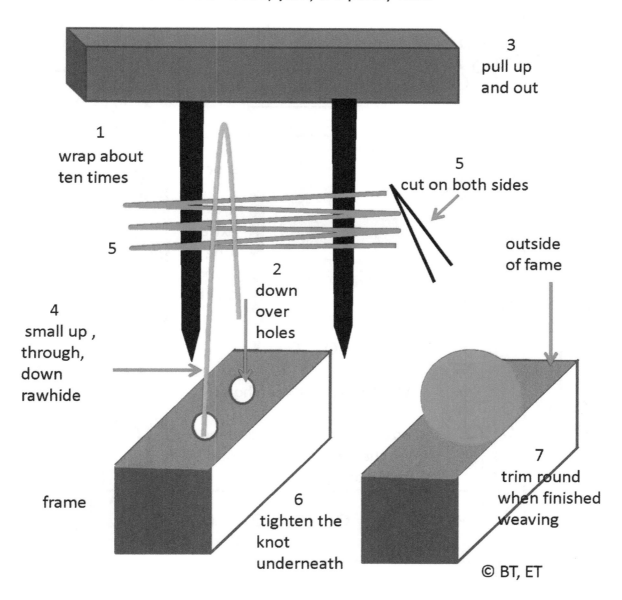

3
pull up
and out

1
wrap about
ten times

5
cut on both sides

5

2
down
over
holes

4
small up ,
through,
down
rawhide

outside
of fame

frame

6
tighten the
knot
underneath

7
trim round
when finished
weaving

© BT, ET

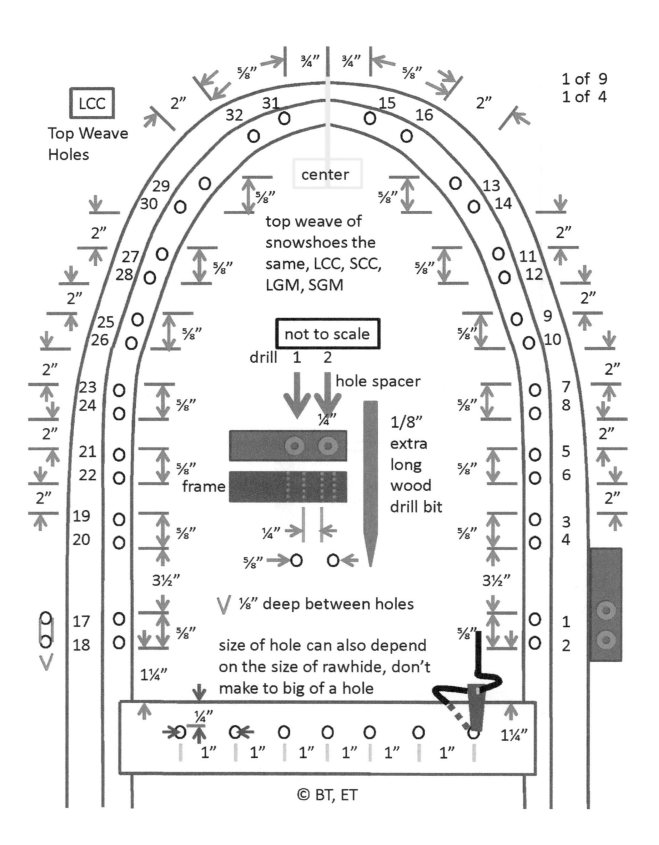

LCC
Top Weave Holes

¾" ¾"
⅝" ⅝"
2" 2"

32 31 15 16

center

29
30

⅝" ⅝"

top weave of snowshoes the same, LCC, SCC, LGM, SGM

13
14

2" 2"

27
28

⅝" ⅝"

11
12

2" 2"

not to scale

25
26

⅝" ⅝"

drill 1 2

hole spacer

9
10

2" 2"

23
24

⅝" ⅝"

1/8" extra long wood drill bit

¼"

frame

7
8

2" 2"

21
22

⅝" ⅝"

¼"

⅝"

5
6

2" 2"

19
20

⅝" ⅝"

3
4

2"

3½" 3½"

∨ 1/8" deep between holes

17
18

⅝" ⅝"

1
2

size of hole can also depend on the size of rawhide, don't make to big of a hole

1¼"

¼"

1" 1" 1" 1" 1" 1"

1¼"

© BT, ET

142

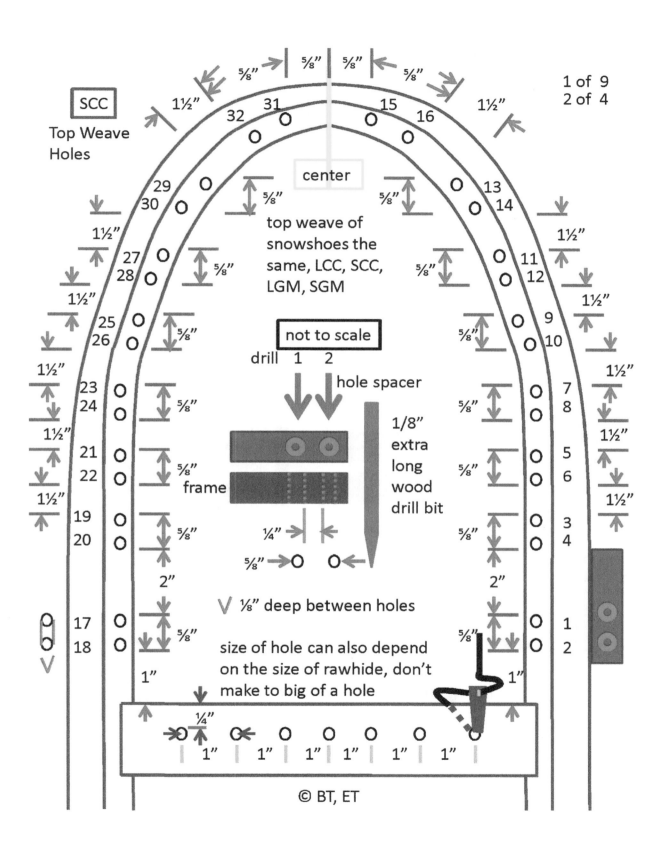

SCC
Top Weave Holes

⁵⁄₈" ⁵⁄₈" ⁵⁄₈" ⁵⁄₈"
1½"   1½"
32 31   15 16

center

29
30   13 14

top weave of
snowshoes the
same, LCC, SCC,
LGM, SGM

1½"   1½"
27   11
28   12

not to scale

25   9
26   10

drill 1 2
hole spacer

1½"   1½"
23   7
24   8
⁵⁄₈"   1/8"   ⁵⁄₈"
extra
long
1½"   wood   1½"
21   drill bit   5
22   6

frame

1½"   1½"
19   3
20   4

¼"
⁵⁄₈" O O
2"   2"

V ⅛" deep between holes
17   1
18   2
⁵⁄₈"   ⁵⁄₈"

size of hole can also depend
on the size of rawhide, don't
make to big of a hole

1"   1"

¼"
→O← O← O O O O O
1" 1" 1" 1" 1" 1"

© BT, ET

143

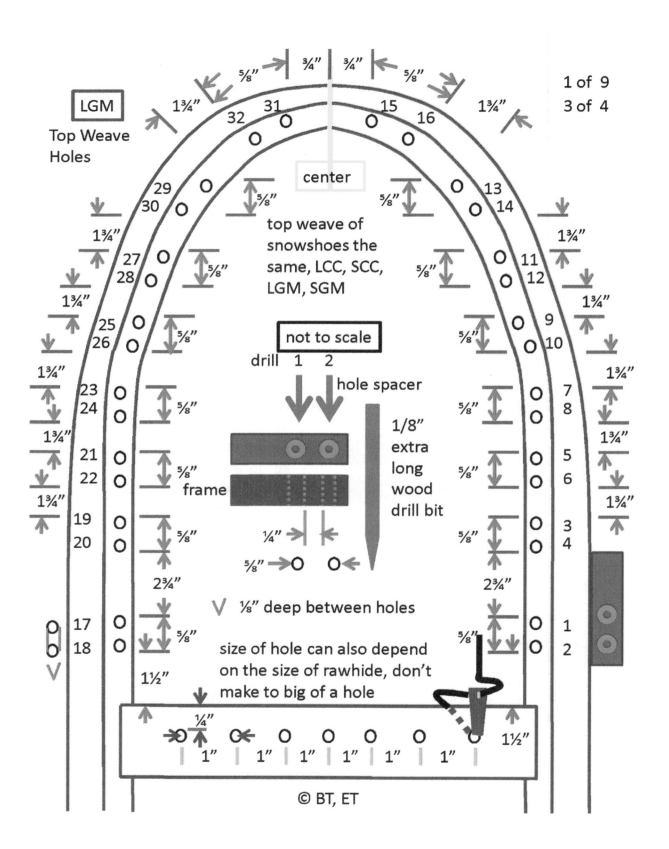

LGM
Top Weave Holes

³⁄₄" ³⁄₄"
⁵⁄₈" ⁵⁄₈"
1³⁄₄" 1³⁄₄"

32 31   15 16

center

29
30

13
14

⁵⁄₈" top weave of snowshoes the same, LCC, SCC, LGM, SGM ⁵⁄₈"

27
28

11
12

not to scale

25
26

drill 1 2

9
10

hole spacer

23
24

frame

7
8

1/8" extra long wood drill bit

21
22

¼"

5
6

⁵⁄₈"

19
20

size of hole can also depend on the size of rawhide, don't make to big of a hole

3
4

2³⁄₄"

⅛" deep between holes

2³⁄₄"

17
18

1
2

1½"

¼"

1½"

1" 1" 1" 1" 1" 1"

© BT, ET

144

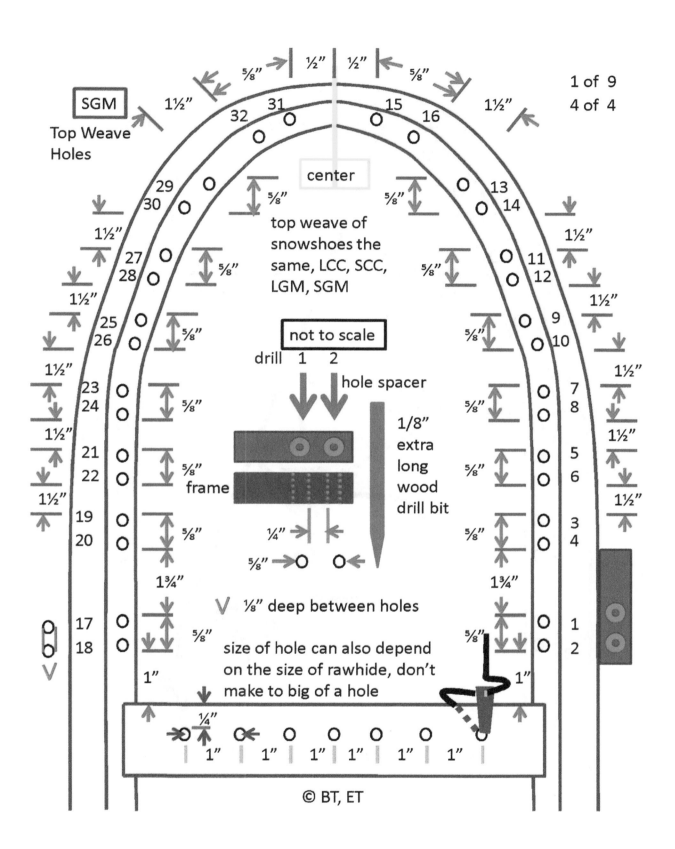

SGM
Top Weave Holes

5/8" 1/2" 1/2" 5/8"
1½"   1½"
32 31   15 16

center

29   13
30   14

top weave of
snowshoes the
same, LCC, SCC,
LGM, SGM

1½" 5/8"   5/8" 1½"

27   11
28   12

not to scale

drill 1 2

25   9
26   10

hole spacer

5/8"   5/8"

1½"   1½"

23   7
24   8

1/8"
extra
long
wood
drill bit

frame

21   5
22   6

1½"   1½"

¼"

5/8" →O   O←

19   3
20   4

⅛" deep between holes

17   1
18   2

1¾"   1¾"

5/8"   size of hole can also depend
on the size of rawhide, don't
make to big of a hole

1"   1"

¼"

→O O← O O O O O

1" 1" 1" 1" 1" 1"

© BT, ET

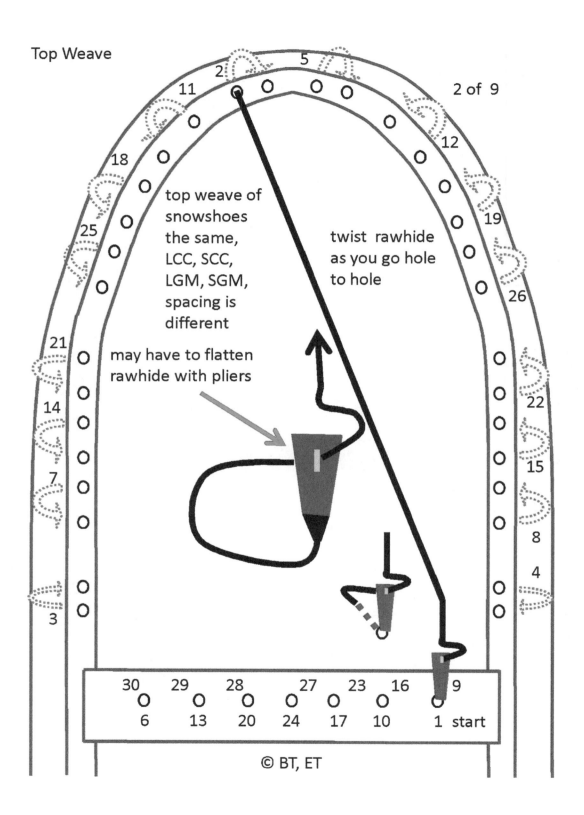

top weave of
snowshoes
the same,
LCC, SCC,
LGM, SGM,
spacing is
different

may have to flatten
rawhide with pliers

twist rawhide
as you go hole
to hole

11 2 5

18

25

12

19

26

21

14

7

22

15

8

4

3

30 29 28 27 23 16 9

6 13 20 24 17 10 1 start

© BT, ET

146

Top Weave

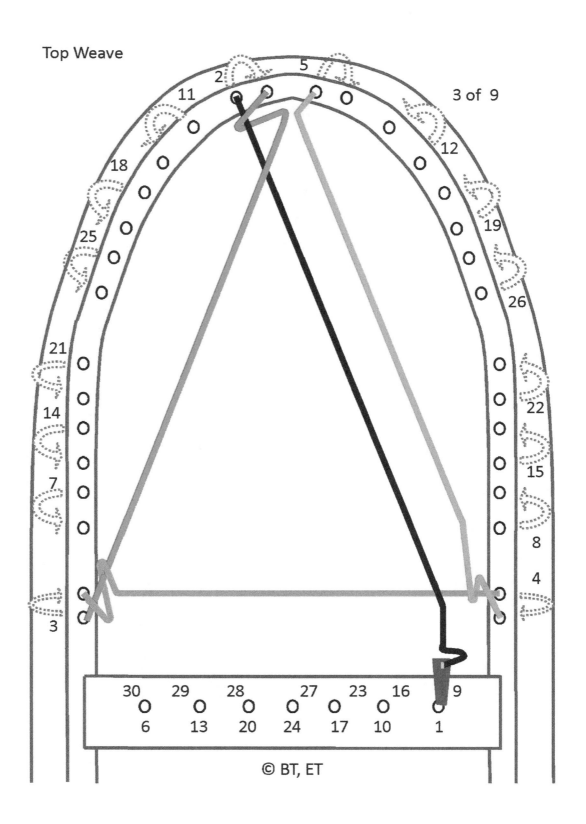

© BT, ET

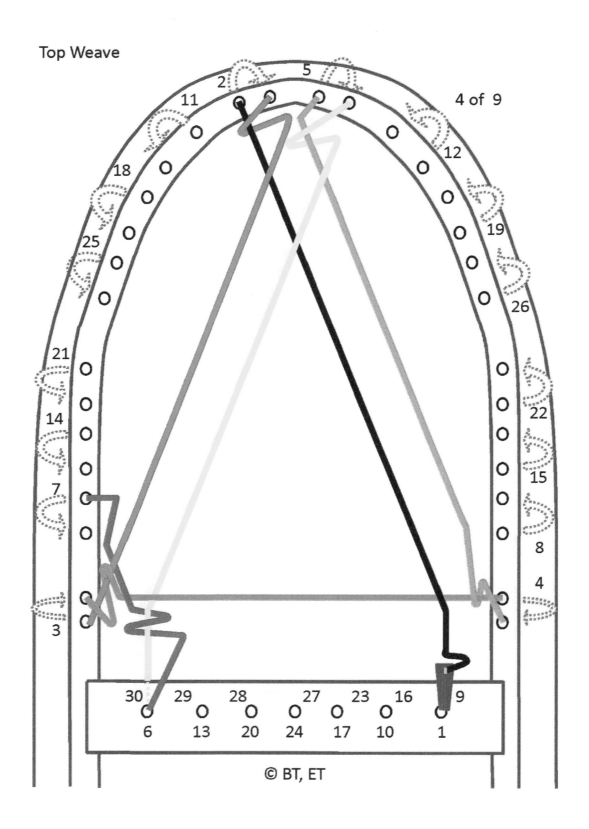

© BT, ET

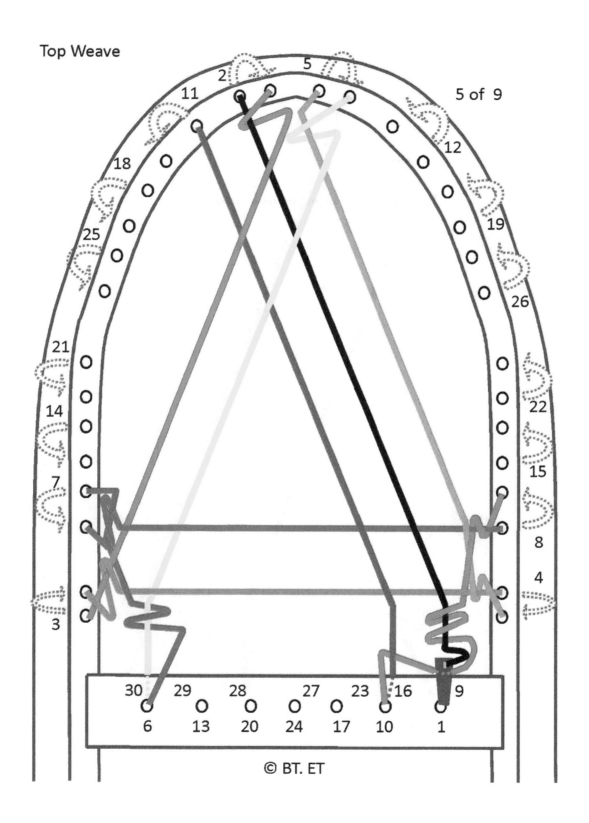

© BT. ET

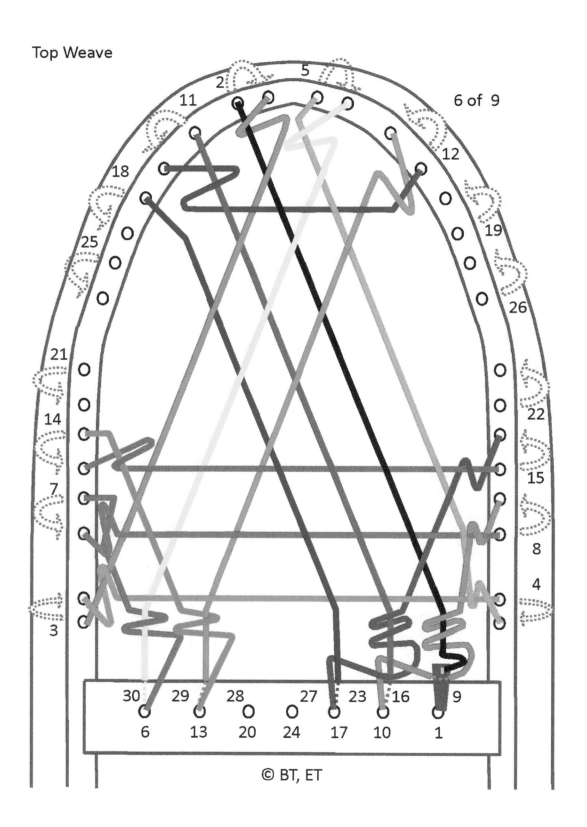

© BT, ET

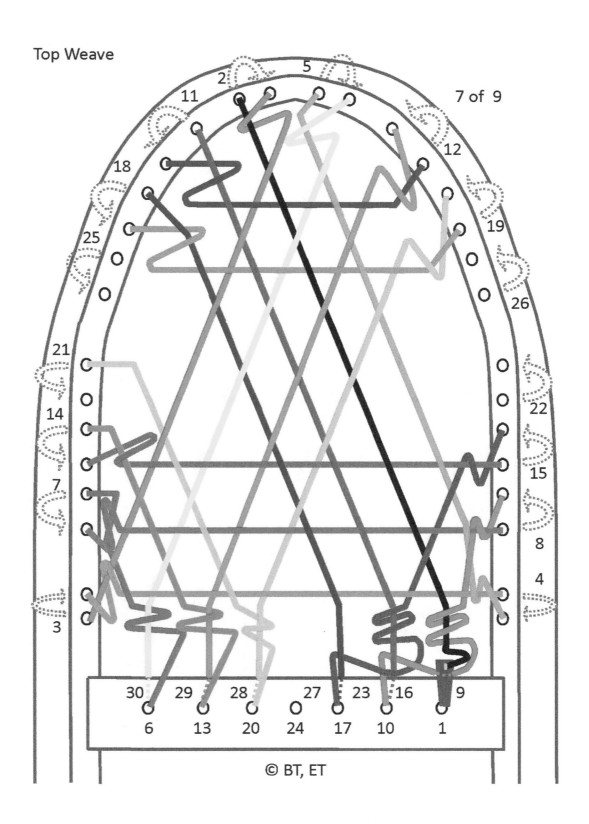

© BT, ET

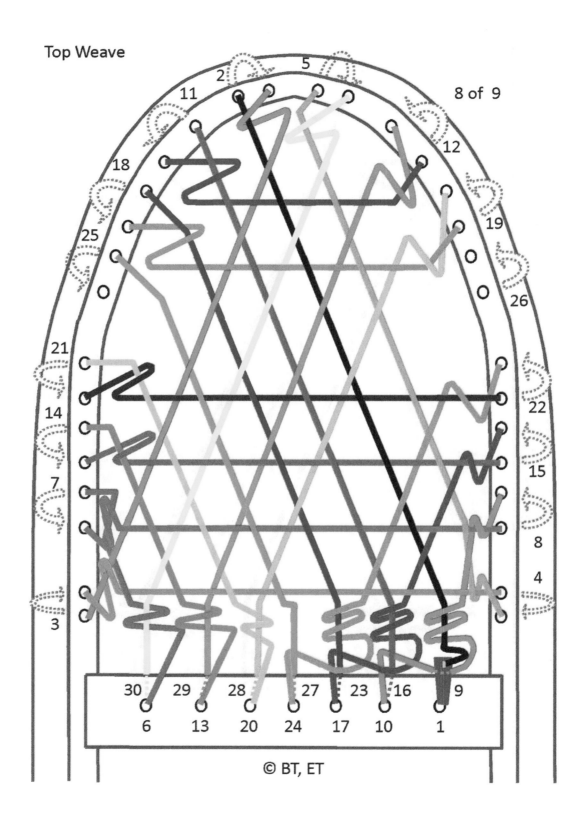

© BT, ET

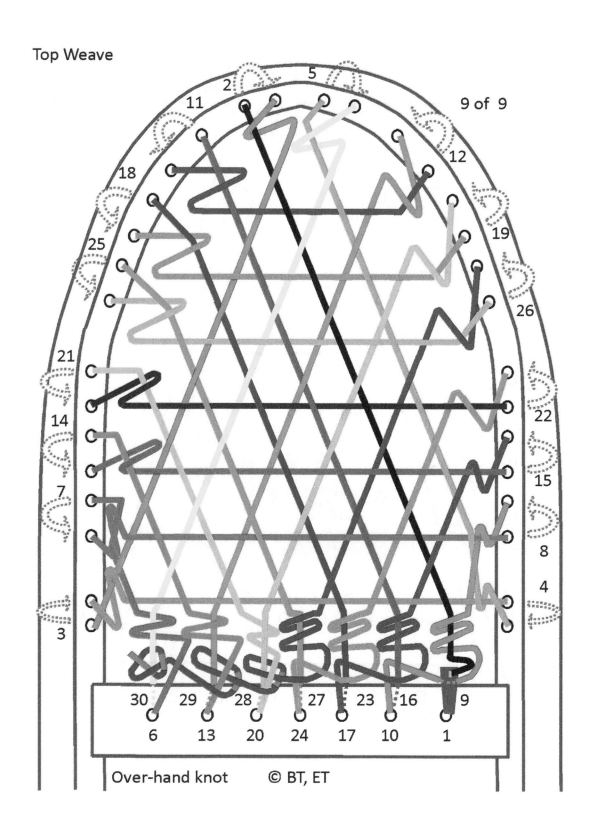

Over-hand knot   © BT, ET

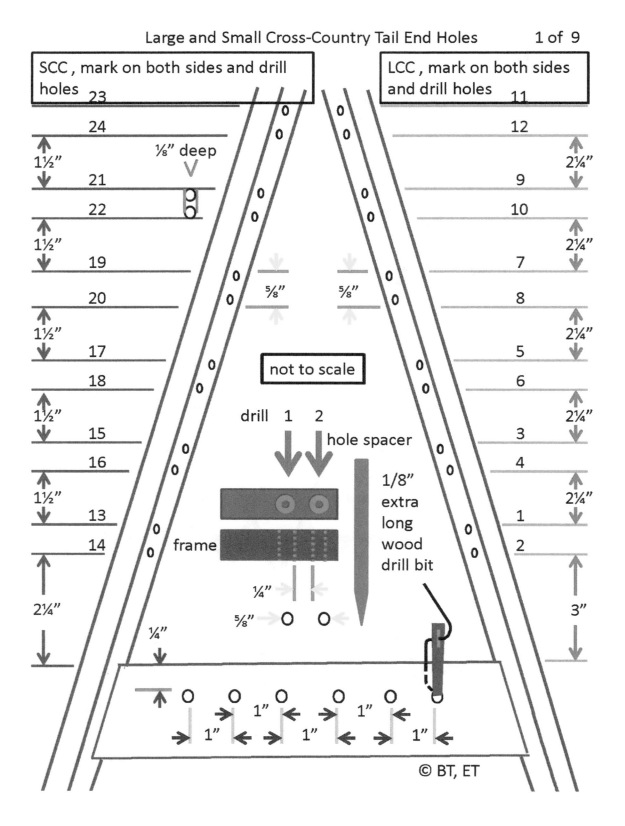

SCC , mark on both sides and drill holes 23

24

1½"

21

22

⅛" deep

1½"

19

20

1½"

17

18

1½"

15

16

1½"

13

14

2¼"

¼"

LCC , mark on both sides and drill holes 11

12

2¼"

9

10

2¼"

7

8

2¼"

5

6

2¼"

3

4

2¼"

1

2

3"

5/8"   5/8"

not to scale

drill   1   2

hole spacer

frame

1/8" extra long wood drill bit

¼"

5/8"

1"   1"

1"   1"   1"

154

© BT, ET

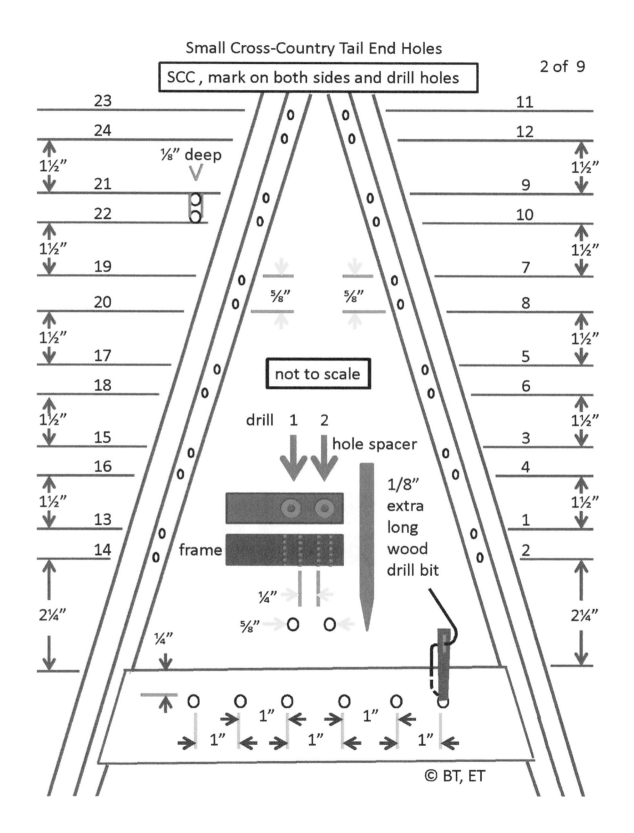

SCC , mark on both sides and drill holes

23

24

1½"

⅛" deep

21

22

1½"

19

⅝" ⅝"

20

1½"

17

not to scale

18

1½"

drill 1 2

15

hole spacer

16

1½"

1/8" extra long wood drill bit

13

frame

14

¼"

¼"

2¼"

⅝"

11

12

1½"

9

10

1½"

7

8

1½"

5

6

1½"

3

4

1½"

1

2

2¼"

1"

1" 1" 1"

© BT, ET

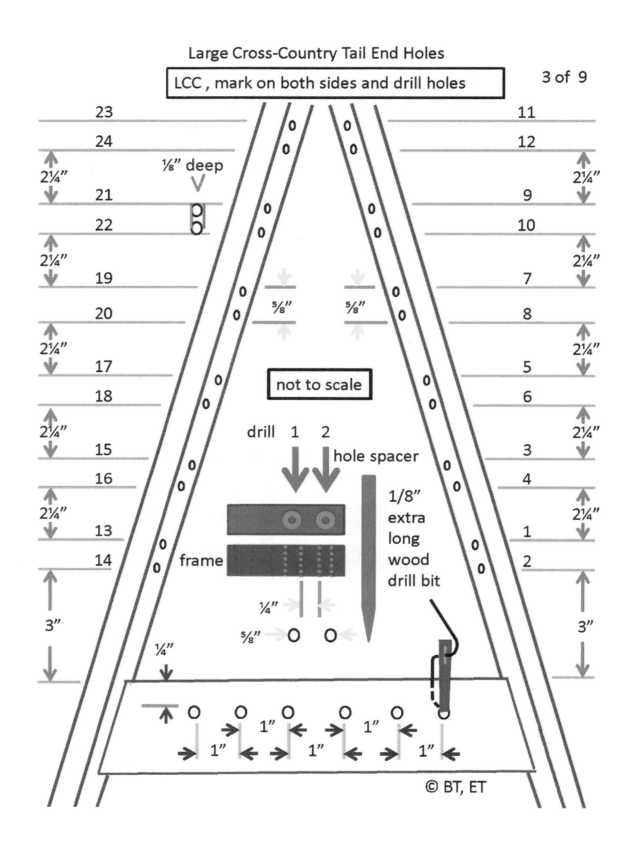

© BT, ET

156

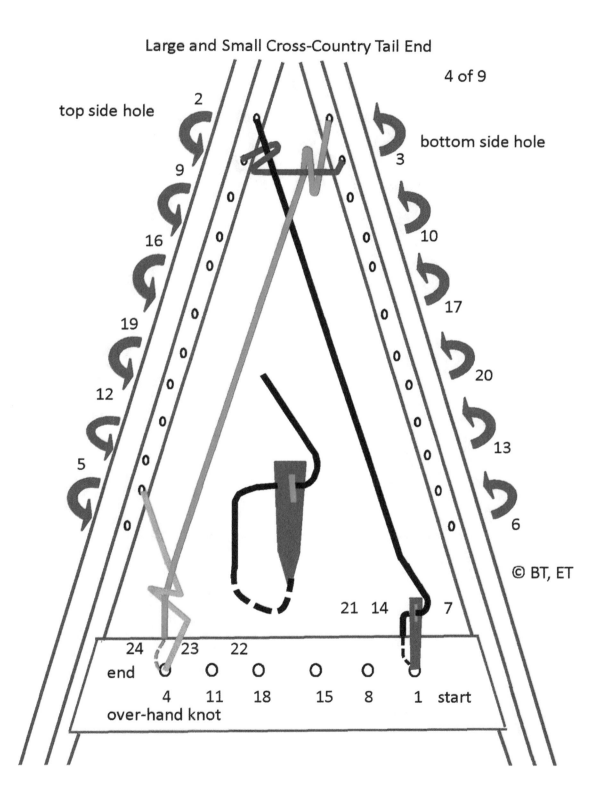

Large and Small Cross-Country Tail End

top side hole

bottom side hole

2

9

16

19

12

5

3

10

17

20

13

6

21 14 7

24 23 22

end

4 11 18 15 8 1 start

over-hand knot

© BT, ET

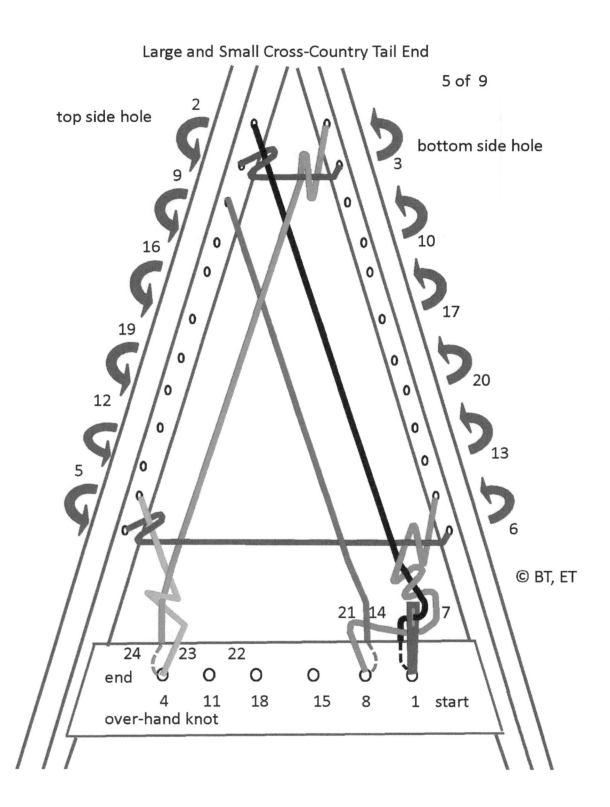

top side hole

bottom side hole

© BT, ET

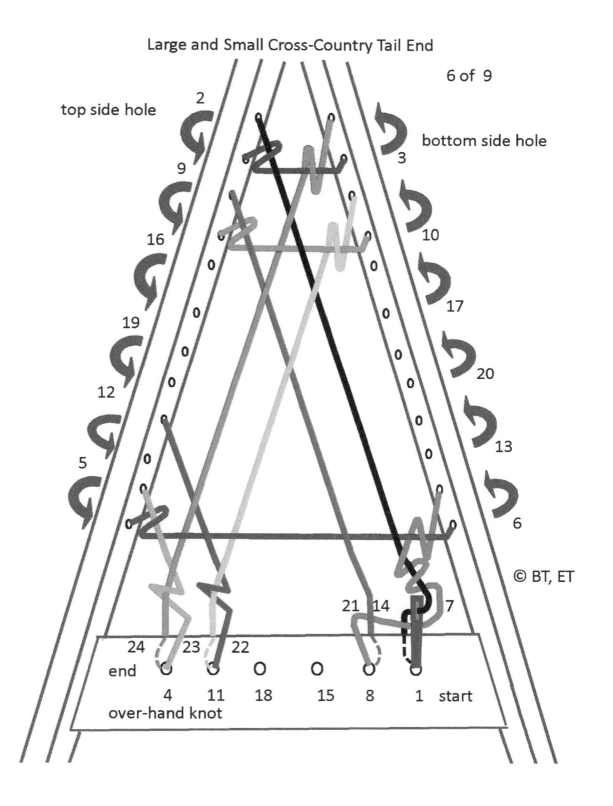

top side hole

bottom side hole

2

9

16

19

12

5

3

10

17

20

13

6

21 14 7

24 23 22

end

4 11 18 15 8 1 start

over-hand knot

© BT, ET

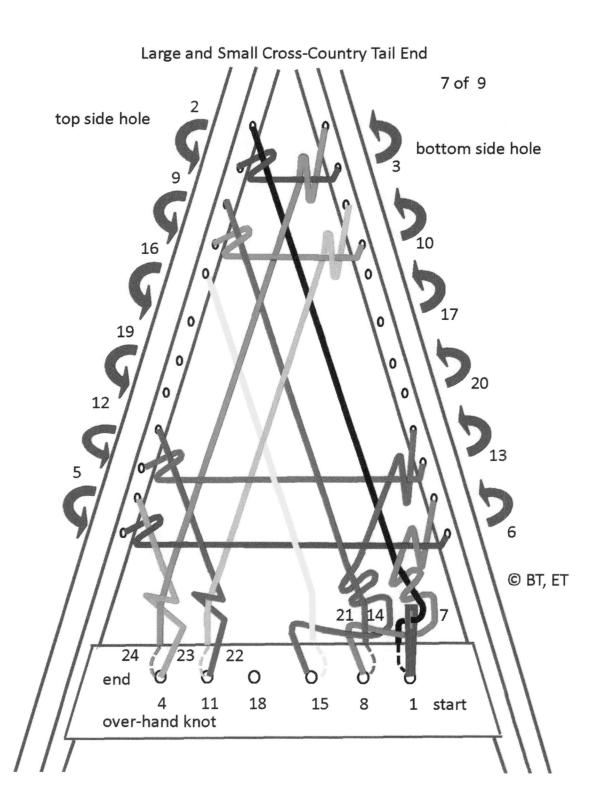

top side hole

bottom side hole

2

9

16

19

12

5

3

10

17

20

13

6

© BT, ET

21 14 7

24 23 22

end

4 11 18 15 8 1 start

over-hand knot

160

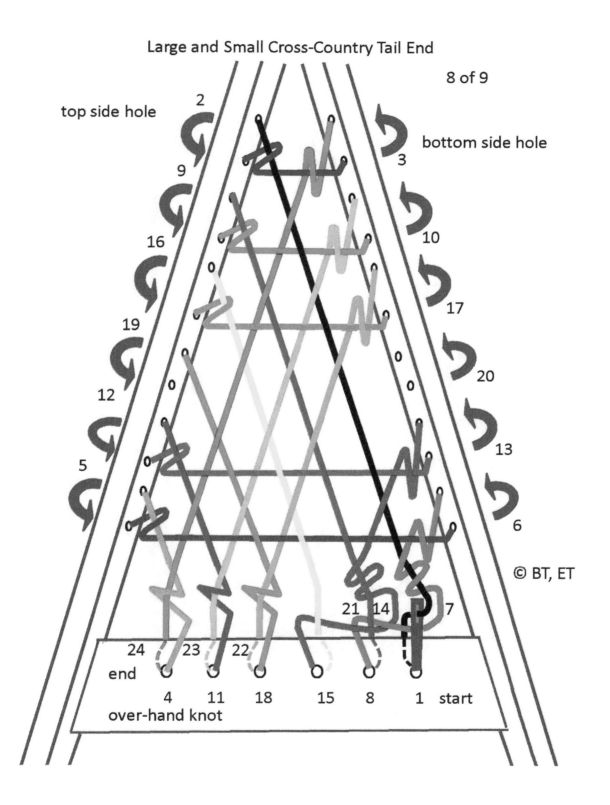

Large and Small Cross-Country Tail End

top side hole

bottom side hole

2

9

16

19

12

5

3

10

17

20

13

6

© BT, ET

21 14 7

24 23 22

end

4 11 18 15 8 1 start

over-hand knot

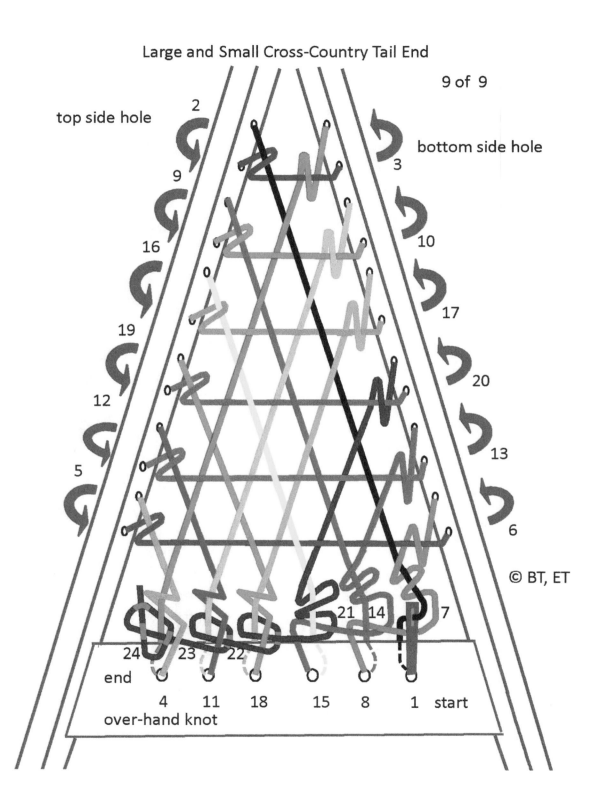

top side hole

bottom side hole

2

9

3

16

10

19

17

12

20

5

13

6

© BT, ET

21 14 7

24 23 22

end

4   11   18   15   8   1 start

over-hand knot

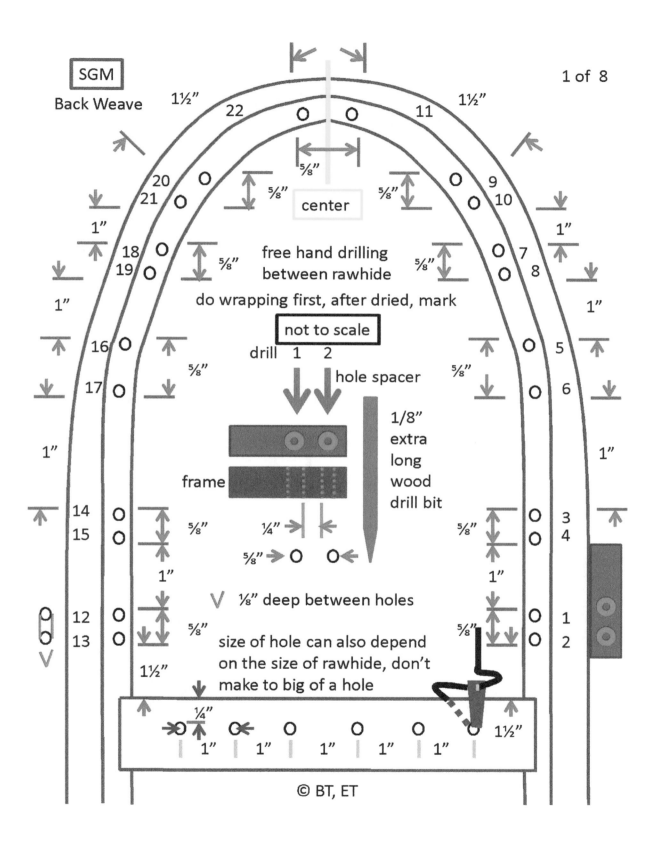

SGM
Back Weave

1½"   22   O O   11   1½"

⅝"
center

20
21

free hand drilling
between rawhide

do wrapping first, after dried, mark

18
19   ⅝"

not to scale

drill   1   2

16   hole spacer

17

1/8"
extra
long
wood
drill bit

frame

¼"

⅝" O   O

V   ⅛" deep between holes

14
15

size of hole can also depend
on the size of rawhide, don't
make to big of a hole

12
13

1½"

¼"

1"   1"   1"   1"   1"   1½"

9
10

7
8

5

6

3
4

1
2

© BT, ET

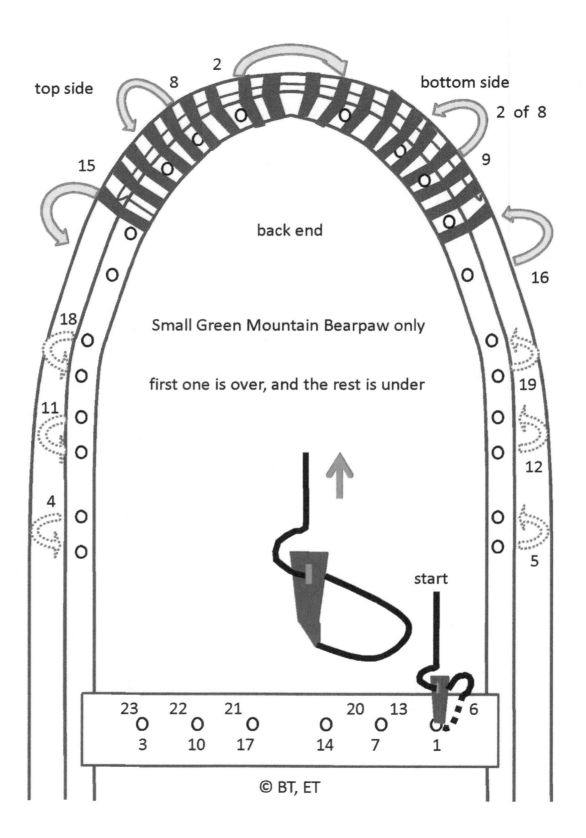

top side

bottom side

back end

Small Green Mountain Bearpaw only

first one is over, and the rest is under

start

© BT, ET

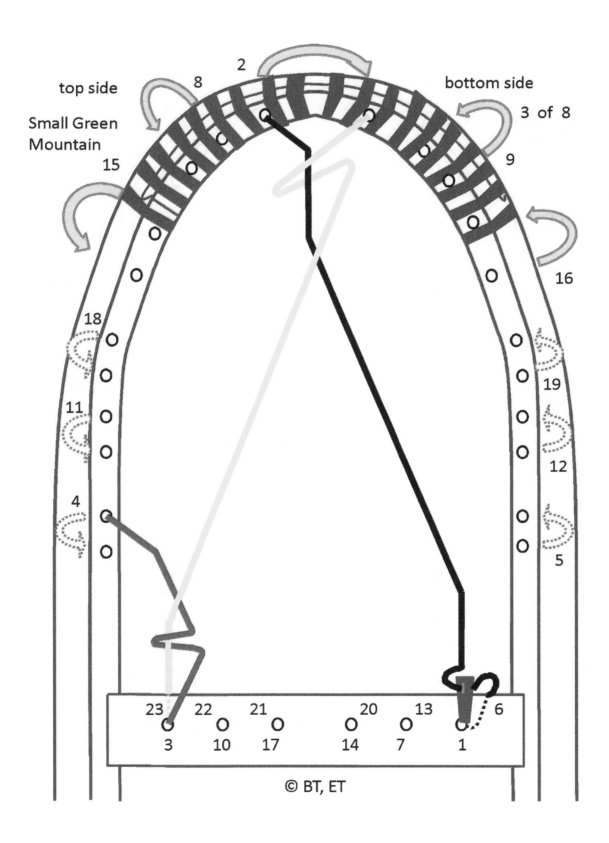

top side

bottom side

Small Green
Mountain

© BT, ET

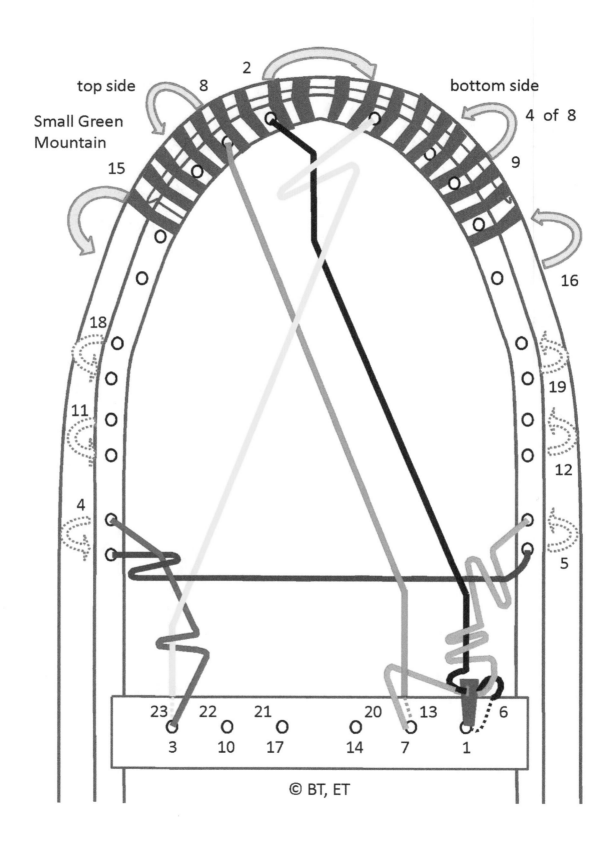

top side

bottom side

2

8

4 of 8

Small Green
Mountain

15

9

18

16

11

19

4

12

5

23　22　21　20　13　6

3　10　17　14　7　1

© BT, ET

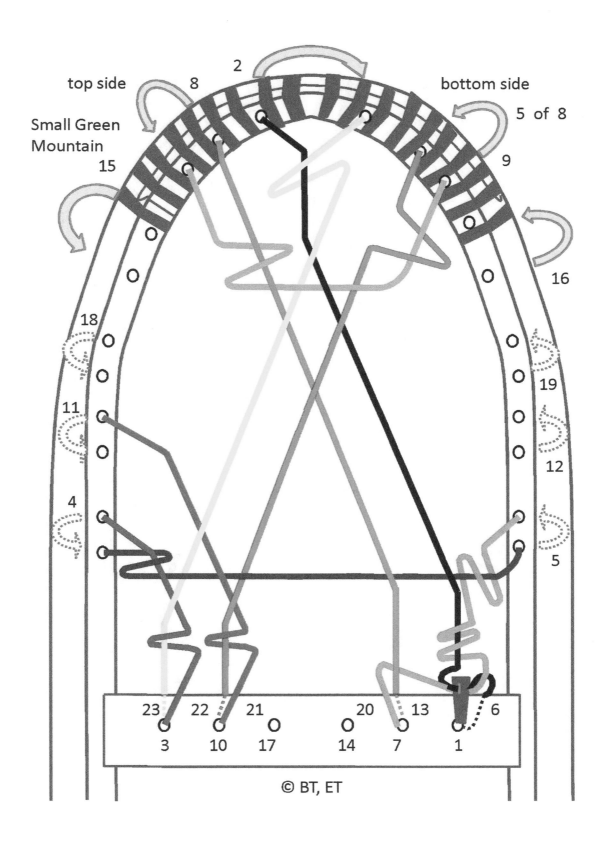

top side

bottom side

Small Green
Mountain

© BT, ET

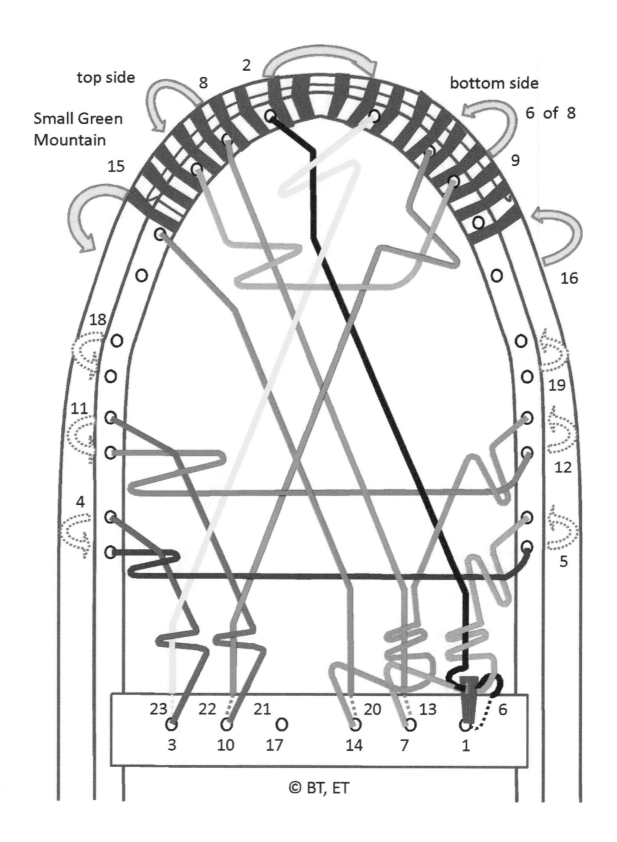

top side

bottom side

Small Green
Mountain

6 of 8

© BT, ET

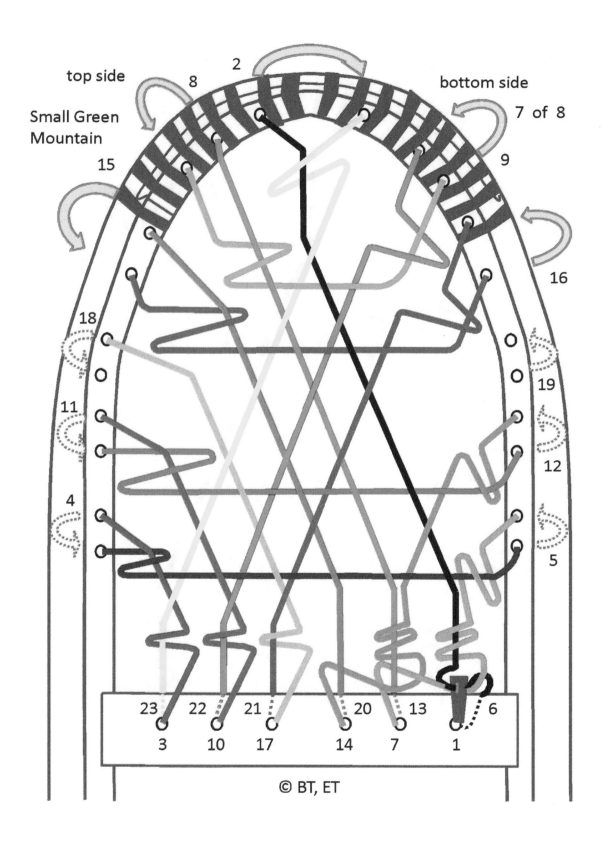

top side

bottom side

8

2

7 of 8

Small Green
Mountain

9

15

16

18

19

11

12

4

5

23 22 21 20 13 6

3 10 17 14 7 1

© BT, ET

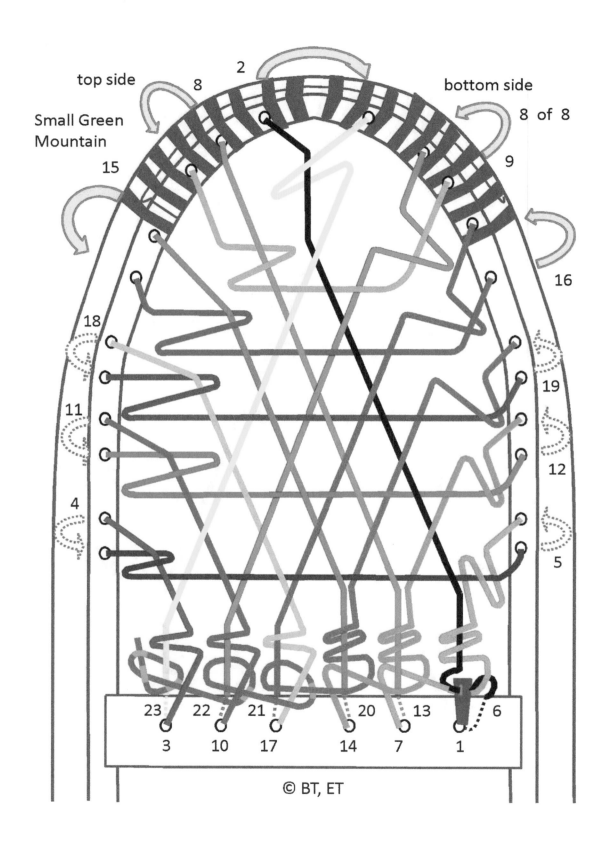

top side

bottom side

Small Green
Mountain

8 of 8

© BT, ET

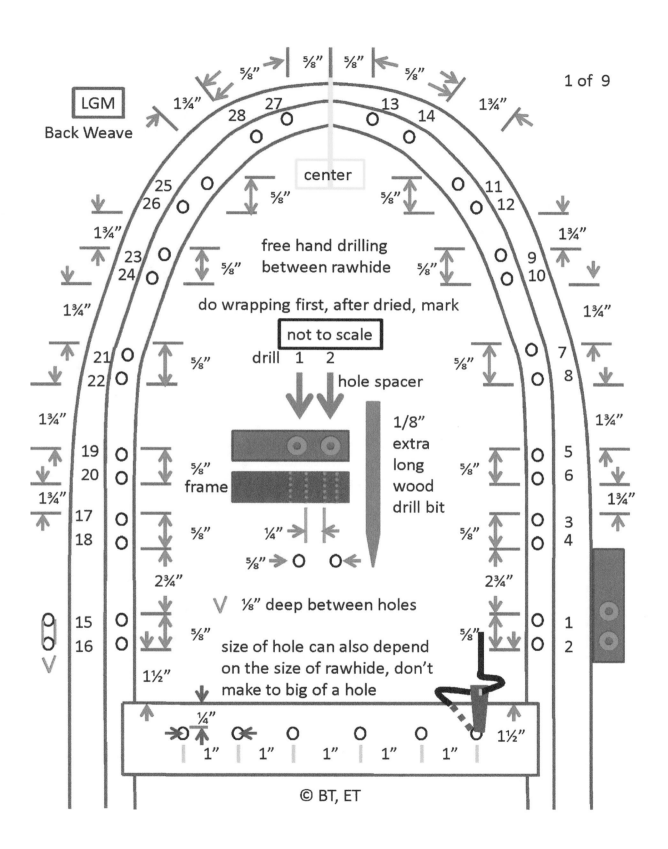

LGM
Back Weave

center

free hand drilling
between rawhide

do wrapping first, after dried, mark

not to scale

drill   1   2
hole spacer

1/8"
extra
long
wood
drill bit

frame

1/8" deep between holes

size of hole can also depend
on the size of rawhide, don't
make to big of a hole

© BT, ET

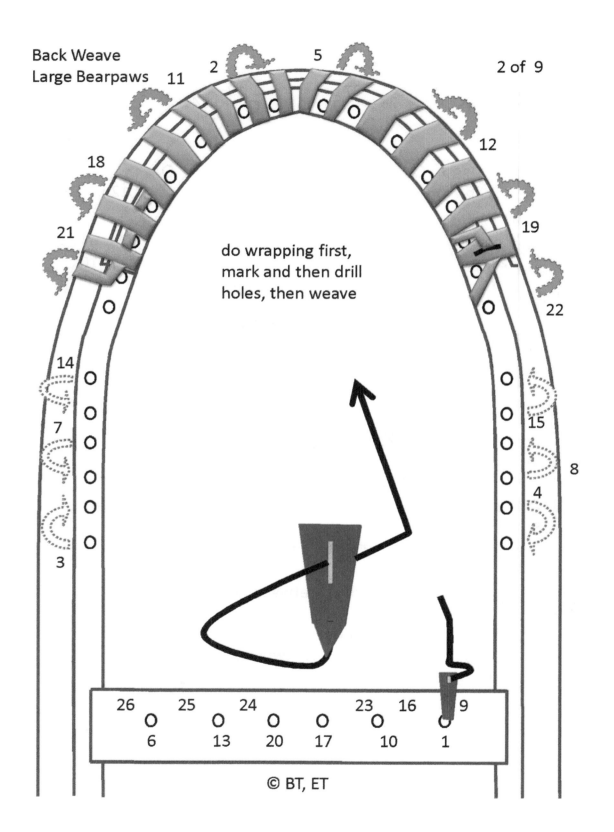

Back Weave
Large Bearpaws

do wrapping first,
mark and then drill
holes, then weave

© BT, ET

172

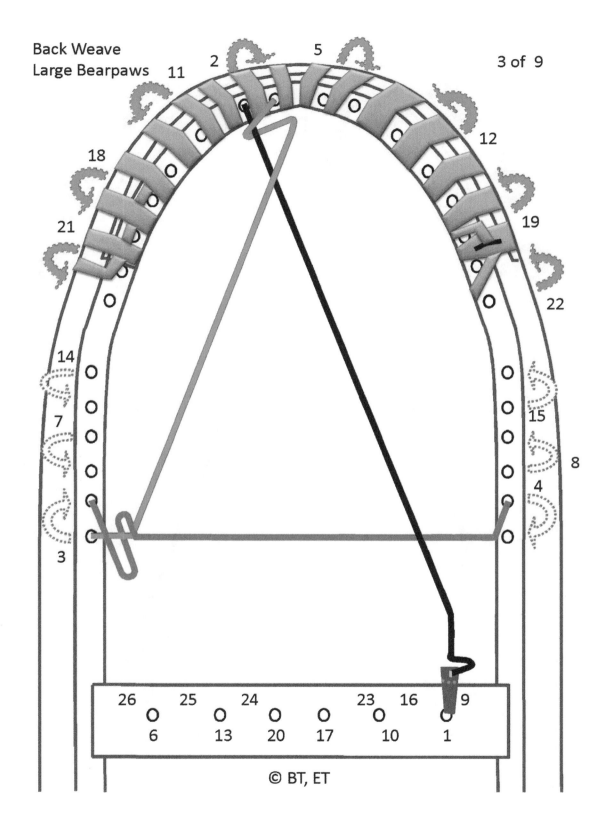

Back Weave
Large Bearpaws

© BT, ET

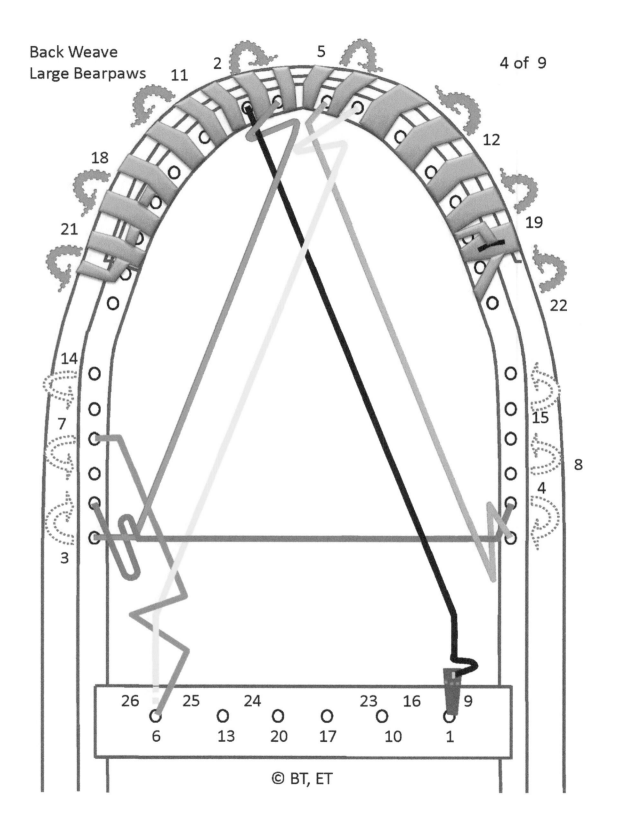

Back Weave
Large Bearpaws

© BT, ET

Back Weave
Large Bearpaws

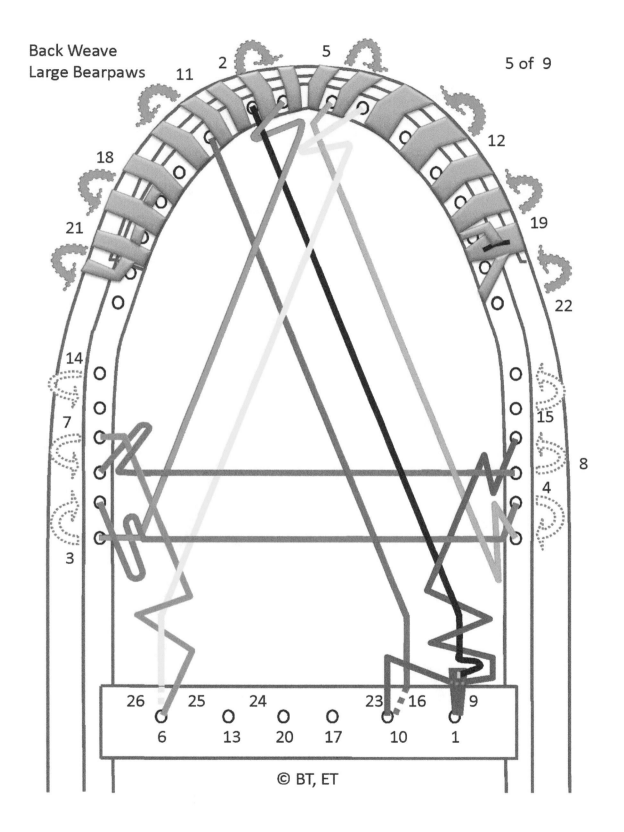

© BT, ET

Back Weave
Large Bearpaws

© BT, ET

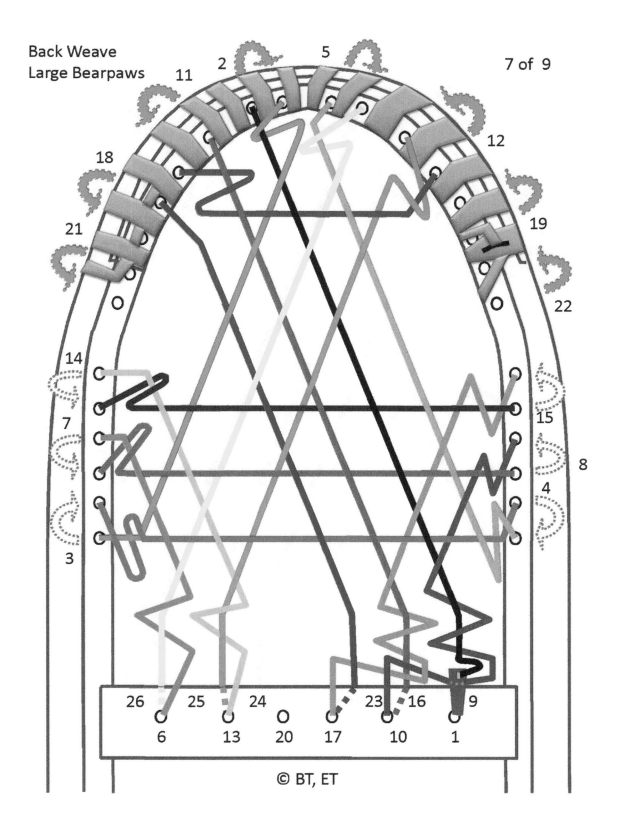

© BT, ET

Back Weave
Large Bearpaws

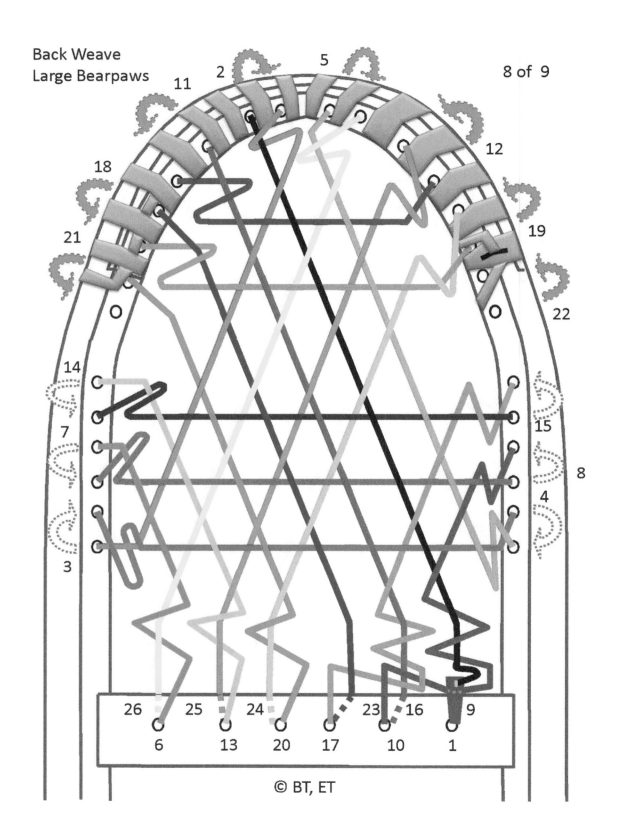

© BT, ET

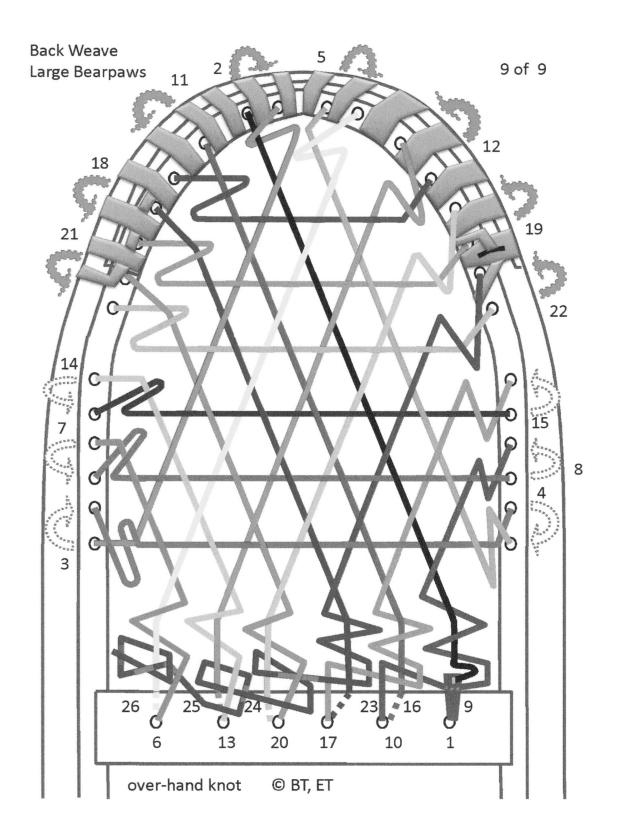

over-hand knot   © BT, ET

Notes:

Part 3 - Now and Future

Chapter 8 - Care of snowshoes

Snowshoes will last two lifetimes and more, if you take care of them. Storing the snowshoes is one of the keys to keeping them in good shape. Rawhide is very strong when dry, but will rot if kept damp for long periods of time. Keep your snowshoes dry as much as you can. It is even better to have a second pair, alternating between them, to allow them sufficient time to dry.

Extreme heat or open flame can be damaging to snowshoe rawhide. Putting them too close to a wood stove or campfire will weaken the fibers. The heat will break down the glue that holds the fibers together and will weaken the strands, making them more easly to break. If you expose your snowshoes to direct heat, you might ask yourself afterward, "Why are they falling apart?"

Also, many times, snowshoes are not put away correctly, and the mice get at them in storage. Always make sure animals or bugs cannot get to them. Hang them from a string or high on a nail, to help keep away from animals, in a garage or where you store them. Animals like to

chew or eat rawhide, which damages the rawhide and even the wood. When dogs are given rawhide, they chew right through it.

The racks are pieces of wood held together by nuts and bolts. They fit tightly on your snowshoes, when you are storing them. They are very important because they keep your snowshoes in their curved shape. It helps them to retain their mold form, which is what is needed to walk in deep snow. If the racks are not used, the snowshoes tend to return to a flat shape over time, which will cause more snow to be carried on the front end of your snowshoe. You do not want to be shoveling snow as you walk!

Keeping the snowshoes covered with environment-friendly varnish is very important. It gives a new look for snowshoes. Just a few brushed on coats are needed on the spots that are used the most, usually, right under the turned up part of the front end of the snowshoes and the dragging bottom of the back ends. Do not make snowshoes too heavy by using too much varnish. When walking on something like rocks or tar, you can spoil your snowshoes. A hard snow crust, dirt, and rocks really wear the snowshoes. If the snowshoe is built too small for the person, pressure is created on the rawhide and wood

frames. Be careful! They are worth a lot, especially, if you are depending on them to get you in and out of the woods.

Care of Bindings

You need to keep bear grease on leather bindings to keep the leather lubricated and in good shape. Mink oil can be used instead of bear grease, but they both work well. Melting the bear fat down slowly, with cedar scent added, as it warms up, makes the best bear grease. It gives a long life to leather. Bear grease, put in jars, will keep for many years. When needed for use, heat the grease a little in a container with water, in a metal pan, on the stove. When the grease is soft, put some on the leather with a cotton cloth. Outside is best place for this type of work. Take the bindings off the snowshoes to apply the oil on. Once or twice a year is good, unless you use them all the time. Always just put a light coat on the binding, so that the leather will not dry rot. If the buckles are rusted and look bad, replace them before they break. Test your bindings by pulling on them, while you have them in your hands.

Purchasing

You really have to check snowshoes out before buying them because there is a difference. Nylon rope is hard to use and will be all cut up on the crust. It does not look good and you do not have a bounce when you walk on them. Cow rawhide is by far the best material. Sawed wood is not as strong because it is dried and steamed to be bent over the mold and let dry. The grain, at places, shoots out and cannot take as much pressure. They make weak snowshoes. There is a difference! You might not notice immediately, but it will become apparent when you are out in the woods, where your life may depend on the quality of your snowshoes.

Fixing Broken Snowshoes/Crosspieces

(Reminder - Do not step on crosspieces.) A spreader bar tool, wood piece helper, can be used to replace crosspieces. With care, spread the frame, take out the broken crosspiece, and put a new one in its place. The spreader bar has two ½ inch dowels placed in a spruce piece of wood, 2 by 8 by 8 inches. The dowels are spaced 1½ inches apart at the ends. Add a piece of wood at the other end of the 2 by 8  inches. A clamp is used to pull apart the frame, with the spreader bar, helping to replace the crosspiece. Do not cut rawhide. Just add a new piece of rawhide through the new crosspiece holes.

Replacing Broken/Bad Rawhide

A jigsaw can be used to remove the old rawhide. Just run jigsaw along the outside of the rawhide next to the frame. Weave a new piece of rawhide on the frame, so that it overlaps on the crosspieces where the rawhide was before. Fixing older snowshoes is quite a task. When you run into an old pair of snowshoes, you want to keep the integrity of the original maker, and yet still make them serviceable. Before fixing the snowshoe, try to write down how to weave the rawhide at the ends, so that you can redo it in a comparable fashion. The center can be woven our way because it is the best and strongest way. The ends may not have the holes in the right place for our weaving. You can do the one hole method at the top/bottom ends, putting yarn or hair on the outside to make it durable. If they are really old, I might not do anything to them. I would leave them alone, just for their looks, and hang them on the wall.

Tips

1.   People should take care of their snowshoes so that they are ready when they are needed. When your life depends on it, it is even more important to have them ready to go.
2.   Lending your snowshoes is not a good idea, because others may not take care of them. When you need them, they may not be available.
3.   Store your snowshoes in a dry area away from too much moisture or heat.
4.   Hang the snowshoes away from where animals can get to them.
5.   Make sure that, while storing your snowshoes, you keep the racks on them, to keep the curve in them.
6.   Renew your snowshoes with a high gloss finish as needed.
7.   Make sure you are not stepping on the crosspieces. Because people nowadays wear big boots, the back cross pieces may not be back far enough to give space for the boots. The crosspieces do not take the pressure of a heavy person with a pack.

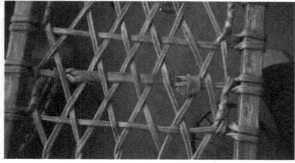

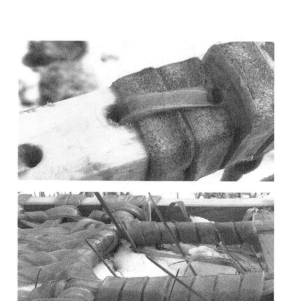

185

Notes:

Chapter 9 – Use of snowshoes

Beaver hat and long coat for cold weather

Snowshoes are not only something I love to make, but are also something I like to use. Snowshoeing in different weather conditions gives me a great feeling of challenge. Feeling the cold apond my face, gives me great satisfaction knowing that I have made the very things that allow me to go on adventures in nature, experiences the average person does not encounter. It is something to be proud of.

Using snowshoes is a great skill and takes time to master. Snowshoeing can be healthful and fun! Put snowshoes on young people, and you will see something exciting happening. They will be challenged to pass through different types of snow. They will breath heavily of the cold fresh air. They may play games or just leave tracks over the unbroken blanket of snow. Can you imagine trying to play tag without tripping up? It takes skill and control. Snowshoeing, when you take part, is a way of life, a way to live, a way we are all connected, even if we live on different sides of the world. Languages are sometimes barriers, but when we put snowshoes on, we are all equal on the snow-covered ground.

Snowshoeing is like walking on a white cloud, and it's a great feeling. You can try hopping over branches as you walk. You can glide or drag your snowshoes in some types of snow. You might just jump because the snow is deep. You can walk sideways as you go up or down a hill. You might try sliding downhill, leaning back not to fall and slide downwards. The important element is to control your balance. When the snow is mostly hard packed, you can run right over the snow. Breaking trails can be a lot of work, but this helps to tap the path for the next person.

Going through narrow places between trees can sometimes be difficult. You might take a step with one snowshoe at a time, in front of the other, to limit the space you need and improve maneuverability. Types of bear-paws are often easier for going through tight spots. Long snowshoes make walking on ice safer because it spreads your weight, but you need to still be careful if the ice is too thin. (Always check the thickness of the ice before snowshoeing on it.) The distribution of weight also helps in deeper snow. You might put canvas at the tail end, to limit the brush getting into the back weaving. This may prevent you from tripping, if hooked on a branch. When hunting, you will want to walk lightly, so that animals cannot hear you. There are many considerations when you walk on snow: reasons for going snowshoeing, the weather conditions, and the type and depth of the snow. Maple sap collecting in the spring is one of the hardest tests on snowshoes, because sap collectors use them all the time and do not have time to dry them completely.

Snowshoeing, as a past time, has skyrocketed with the increased interest in health and exercise. Your health is important and you have to listen to your heart and lungs when on your snowshoes. Your breathing should be steady and not too fast. People having trouble with their hips or legs should have snowshoes that are narrower to help with the pressure to the body. It may also help if less wood is used, but have them still strong enough to support a person. You should slowly build up the distances, as your endurance increases. Bring safety resources, including food, water, and medical equipment, even for a short walk. Snow is not good to eat unless melted because it uses energy to melt. Try to have somebody with you; it is safer and more fun to snowshoe with others. Let someone know where you are going and when you will be back. Bring something to make a fire. You may think snowshoeing is just fun, but if you go into the woods, be ready for the unexpected. Preparation in different environments can save your life.

Be careful when going downhill. It is easy to fall, partly because you may be going fast, and it is harder to stop. Lean back when walking, so that if you fall, it will be on your snowshoes, and you can get up quickly. When walking on snowshoes, balance is very important. Keep a slow steady pace and keep your hands ready to help stabilize you to prevent falling. Free hands will help keep your balance and support an unintentional landing in the snow. I lean back, bend my knees, and keep low to the ground for control. You have to be able to remove snowshoes fast if you fall and do not want to be trapped in an awkward position. Be cautious not to twist your foot. A foot or ankle injury could hinder your ability to get back, so keep safety in mind. The tail of the snowshoes helps you balance. It is like a rudder that helps to keep the front up and line up to keep moving straight. You can add weight if the snowshoes need it. That is why we build them the way we do; you will have fewer problems and they will balance better. The fronts should stay above the snow, allowing the snow to stay on the ground and not on your snowshoes.

Snowshoe poles can be used, but be careful if you use them in deep snow. The unknown depth of the snow, like snow covered branches, can confuse you and give less support than what you expect, especially in softer snow. There are also wild animals in fields and woods. Take care in the woods and keep an eye out for them. Check ice thickness with a wooden or metal rod ice pick, and take extra care on unfamiliar trails and in deep snow.

One of the best clothing considerations, for winter weather and heat, is layering. Wool was used because of its warmth. Even if it wet, it tends not to freeze and your sweat breathes through the wool. Wool is best to keep out the moisture and to dry more quickly. Dress in layers so you can remove them quickly and easily if needed. You do not want to be too cold or so hot that you overheat. Just like any other outdoor sport, it is important to keep the outside temperature and wind factor in mind. When it is cold, it does not take much time to freeze up. Keep walking! You will be exercising as you walk, causing your body to keep toasty. Warm boots are a must for long walks. Elastic top leggings that go over all the bottom of your pants, over your boot tops, will help to keep snow and ice from getting into your boots. There should be a strap going under your boot to help divert deep snow. It looks good and also helps to prevent the brush from hitting your leg. Wet snow will not stick and get into your boots.

If dragging a sled, keep it away from the ends of your snowshoes. Be careful when walking with dogs as well. A dog can also jump onto the back of your snowshoes and may trip you. If you are alone, take extra caution. You can never afford to be careless out in the woods. If you get hurt, it takes time to get back or for others to reach you when you are unable to walk. Keep an eye on snow loads in trees or branches. Snow can fall on you when branches are moved. Things can easily happen, so be careful and tell someone where you are going and when you will be back.

Snowshoes can be useful tools, even when they are not strapped to your feet. You could use your snowshoes as a chair if you had to sit down, rather than getting wet by sitting on the

snow. Stand on both snowshoes vertically and deeply in the snow, making sure they are solid so you do not fall over. Also, just sit down on a flat snowshoe and use the other as a table. Snowshoes can also be used to remove snow at times when needed; they make handy shovels, especially when the snow is soft and light. These are some of the usages of snowshoes, besides walking on the snow.

Good bindings are important to keep your feet secure as you walk. Hinge-bindings work well because they do not allow any ice or snow build up under your boots. Keep an eye on them! Always keep a string handy for a quick repair if something happens.

Snowshoes are not just snowshoes! They have to work like snowshoes and last under harsh conditions. The rawhide has to be the true thickness because split rawhide is weaker. The squareness of the wood frame is best because it grabs and cuts through the snow and helps grip as you are walking in the snow. Also the frames help hold the center rawhide tight and in place, making that also into a grip, like chains on tires of vehicles. The tips of the snowshoes are raised for a few reasons, like going downhill easily. Flat snowshoes tend to make you fall forward. Flatter snowshoes tend to catch the crust and trip you up. Curved snowshoes also hold you up more on the deep snow. It is not that much harder to put a bigger bend on the front ends. Everything on the snowshoe has a purpose. We, as master snowshoes makers, need to continually consider and evaluate our process.

In the middle of the snowshoes, there is a small upward bend in the wood to give a spring to your steps, a bounce that can make it easier for you to walk. Make sure that the bend stays there when you put them into a rack. You may have to put something in the center for that bend. Running with these snowshoes is easy and fast. Just the right width makes your snowshoes better adapted for walking and running, for each person. For racing, I would make them lighter, with less wood and finer rawhide. There are many different ways to use snowshoes, depending on what you are planning to do with them.

Tips

1. Keep safety in mind when you are snowshoeing. Today, hunter orange is needed so people can see you even if you are on a trail. Never wear white mittens when you are out doors, because it could be taken for a deer's tail.

2. Inspect snowshoes before using them in the woods.

3. Even check the other person's snowshoes, because they may not know what to look for. If theirs break, you'll have to help them.

4. It is a good idea to bring food and water with you when snowshoeing. Eating snow will dehydrates you. You can boil the snow into water to drink.

5. Keep a strong string or something to help fix your binding if they break.

6. When walking in the woods, keep some distance between you and your partner. Branches can snap backward and cause harm to the person behind.

7. Look up often as you walk. A branch or heavy snow may come down on you, especially if it is really windy.

8. Test your bindings by pulling on the straps to see if they are strong before each usage, especially if you go out in the woods or further from civilization.

9. Replace old or rusty buckles that do not look strong.

10. Protect your eyes from the glare of white snow with sunglasses.

Notes:

Chapter 10 - Continuing Knowledge

Interesting Facts

Other things that you can make with rawhide and ash are furniture, canoe seats, toys

 (lacrosse sticks), axe handles, and crooked knife handles/wrapping. A while back, thin rawhide was even used instead of windows before glass became common. Brown ash wood is beautiful for shelves and cabinets. The baskets that

can be made with the layers, of the tree, are amazing: decorative baskets, pack baskets, potato baskets, creel baskets, laundry baskets, and picnic baskets. These containers are sturdy and allow an air flow. They can be very useful for hiking or carrying items; they are strong and light weight. More fancy baskets with intricate designs can be used for the home.

Joan and Edmond Theriault

Baskets are made from black ash trees.

Woodman, lumberjacks, and other snowshoers would wear bright colors in the woods so people could see them from afar and prevent them from being shot at. It also helped to identify who it was from a distance. Some wore a red silk strip or scarf about the middle of their coat to help the snow from coming up if they fell. Some snowshoers painted their snowshoes red and black or left longer tails for balance or drag. The paint helped them to find the snowshoes if left near trees or on white snow. The natural color of the wood blends in, and with just a little snow on the snowshoes, they could easily be lost. The color could also help see the snowshoes when using an axe or chainsaw, to avoid hitting them. Snowshoers all added their own touch to snowshoes. I think that is great because, most of the time, it showed their uniqueness and creativity.

Hudson Bay – Red and black wool blanket jacket – trade value: 3½ beaver

© Louise Bouchard 2013

Snowshoes that are heavier in the back give more lift to the front. There are things you can do to make the back ends of snowshoes weigh a bit more, like adding wood in-between the two pieces of tail where the frame comes together or move the front crosspieces. This would help with snowshoes that are short. There will be less back end lift. This will help to get a smoother walk and decreases the chance of tripping.

Teaching

Teaching is very important to me. I want to let people know how to make snowshoes. It is not always easy to just tell people how. Guidance with the materials and assistance with the steps, just like any craft, helps to make something wonderful. I enjoy being an active part of teaching others, keeping the knowledge alive. It is fun! I feel the history is ongoing with snowshoes. After they make a pair, you can see it in their eyes. They are proud of what they have done. They become a part of being in the snowshoe makers' guild, which is quite an honor and accomplishment. With time, help, and good direction, it is not too difficult.

In the past, we have taught people the basics of how to make snowshoes. My father has talked at elementary schools in the Fort Kent area for many years, when my brothers and sisters were young. He was a great model for show-and-tell! My father and I have taught individuals how to make their own snowshoes for Adult Ed. at the Fort Kent High School and at the Tech. Center, in Frenchville. This involved getting a lot of materials ready in a short period of time.

Jordan Theriault

Individual snowshoes are one of a kind. Each pair is a little different. You want pairs to match when placed side-by-side, by using similar rawhide cuts at the same time. The first pair of snowshoes weaved is hard on the hands because the rawhide dries quickly. Wet the rawhide a bit here and there, but do not make it too wet. This will make it a little slippery and harder to work. With experimenting and practice, the best moisture level can be achieved. It will become more of an automatic process. Some people put together a fast job and call them traditional, but is that what you want? It takes more than rawhide and wood tied together to make a dependable pair of traditional snowshoes. Once you see how snowshoes are made and use them, they will have more meaning.

Conclusion

I want more people around the world to learn how to make snowshoes, and this sharing of information is a great part of my goal. I would like to have a place where people could come together and talk about making snowshoes. I know they communicate on the internet, I would like to have a chatroom to talk about snowshoes and making them. I enjoy talking with people who want to know more about making snowshoes or using snowshoes. It is difficult to go into too much detail unless they really want to make them. The kids I meet encourage me. I really like talking with them because they are the next generation to share and pass the knowledge. They may just want to learn about snowshoes and using traditional snowshoes, or they may take up snowshoe making.

It seems like there is now a movement to learn and bring the art of traditional snowshoe making alive. The usage is growing fast, but many people are only willing to pay just so much for a pair of snowshoes. I predict that someday, people will be willing to pay more, for a high quality pair of traditional snowshoes. I have been doing all kinds of things to bring snowshoes to life in my own ways. I try to attend all kinds of activities and events to demonstrate and share my knowledge of snowshoes. I have stored my information on a DVD and in this book. I use the internet to reach out to more people. I bring my snowshoes wherever I go. Many people have come up to me and talked about my snowshoes. They tell me they use snowshoes, something about snowshoes, their experiences, or stories about snowshoeing. It feels good to talk about snowshoes year around. It is what I like to do, and it's a great privilege to meet so many people.

I show my snowshoes, carry them with me often, and talk to people. I can be standing by myself near a crowd of people, and they gravitate towards the snowshoes. People are really interested and want to know more. They often want to try snowshoeing. It is so much fun in parades. I have a very positive experience, when I bring them, wherever I go. I take pictures with many people. There can never be too many pictures highlighting our traditional snowshoes. Nowadays, there are many cameras everywhere, especially in cell phones!

© Louise Bouchard 2013

Winning the Traditional Arts Master from the Maine Art Commission in 2005 was a great honor! It is even better the second and third time around. It brings a welcome feeling and shows that I am helping to preserve a valuable Maine tradition. I have been given a third grant focusing on teaching snowshoe making to the next generation, Jordan Labbe, age 12. These grants have helped me to gain credibility regarding my art. With more publicity, people are more interested in how to make them. I hope someday a lot of people around the world will know the stories of our past. These grants were funded in part by a grant from the Maine Arts Commission,

I would like for us to keep these stories alive and to have a museum in which to put snowshoe pictures and models. I would like to have materials that made snowshoes the best invention in the great outdoors. People tell me about others who have made snowshoes. In the presence of a pair of snowshoes, people are willing to open up about all their experiences. Someone told me about one lady called, "snowshoe lady", who used snowshoes a lot.

The key things to remember when making and storing a great pair of snowshoes are: good wood, big strong rawhide, non-moving rawhide, dry storage, and dependable harnesses.

Once you see how snowshoes are made and use them, your appreciation will be greater. One teacher used snowshoes to cross a lake in my area, Eagle Lake, to teach an educational lesson. There are many possibilities because you could feel how it was back then, putting so many miles on them. Many people depend on traditional snowshoes. They are coming back big-time, in some areas, especially for exercising. Having a pair is important because you have something you can use in the deepest of snow conditions. People pass their snowshoes to other family members, along with the stories that go with them!

Some people put together a fast job and call them traditional, but if your life can depend on them, is that what you want? It takes more than rawhide and wood tied together to make a dependable pair of traditional snowshoes. Where there is more meaning is where they have been and all they have done. Many people depended on them; it was who you were, using them all winter long. They were the only way to get around. Few people today know that much about traditional snowshoes or even think about it. The culture has lost a lot because there are not as many snowshoe makers left in the world. Much of the knowledge has not been written, partially because it is difficult to give directions for specific procedures. I think that, if things do not change in the next ten years, we will lose even more. I know, by talking to people and reading information, that the world is changing fast. Just a few books have been written about snowshoes and even less on how to make them. More is mentioned about snowshoeing as an activity in newspapers, articles, and books, not really giving a description of all the work involved in creating them. We sometimes see snowshoes in TV shows or movies.

We need to work hard to keep up with the changes, keeping snowshoe making alive. One step I have taken is to produce a DVD and write this book. In this book, I will try to share

the information that my father and I have discovered, along our "path" of discovery. We have looked at the truth of snowshoe making: from the gross, slimy skin to the wonderfully finished product. There is still much to learn about snowshoes and many adventures yet to be experienced. My father and I have done so much with snowshoes, and we enjoy sharing our knowledge, experiences and techniques with the world. We have had over eighty years of combined learning and expertise, putting in the work and time, to master this talent. This knowledge and skill is very important because it is part of our history and tradition.

I have big dreams for traditional snowshoe making. I do see this knowledge extending beyond the state of Maine, to other states, and other countries including Canada and France. How can I tell it to the world? There is a lot of snow out there, and snowshoeing can help us see and touch a lot of snowflakes. I feel that I need to get out there more and let people know about snowshoes in the best way I can, by sharing my knowledge. I do see some changes, which are good, but there could be so much more. I see a business that could create good paying jobs. It would be a hands-on task to make high quality snowshoes. Snowshoes that are of the highest quality would make the difference. Workers would be much more proud of the work they produced, if the process itself was highly valued.

There are some people who make a few pairs of traditional snowshoes and then they are done. That is okay, but we need people to continue with the craft of snowshoe making. There is even a need for people to fix some of those old snowshoes. Many people ask me to repair their old or broken snowshoes, but I just do not have the time. I would like to sell kits that will instruct people on how to repair their worn or broken snowshoes and show people so they can help me fix them. There is even a skill in fixing very old wooden traditional snowshoes. Not too many people can make these repairs so that the snowshoes match and resemble the original work. My DVD will help with this instruction and hopefully this book will help even more, with the details on measurements, with diagrams and pictures that are labeled to make Theriault's Snowshoes.

I have collected some old snowshoes, but it seems that, a lot of times, I find that the person who made these snowshoes has passed on. All their knowledge is gone and the families do not know what happen to the equipment like molds and tools used to make traditional snowshoes. I travel all around and keep going out to different places to find out more about traditional snowshoes and their makers. Even today, there are not too many collectors. Museums are some of the largest collectors. I have collected just a few pairs and some molds.

There are some carvings, drawing, and paintings of snowshoes, but I have not found many. I know they are out there, but they are difficult to find. When there is snow and it is cold, people will use snowshoes. I take a lot of pictures because I know someday soon, I will be able to put them on the internet or in a books.

I would like to see traditional snowshoes in the Olympics someday soon. This kind of experience would encourage the rewarding sport of snowshoeing. The Winter Games could include an exciting dash or an extended distance run that would encourage people to seriously compete. You can become one of a few, in the world, that can make snowshoes. I hope someday that a lot of people will be making traditional snowshoes and that it will be a big event at for the Olympics. We need to keep traditional snowshoes in the light.

I have been on the Bill Green Maine show. In my DVD, I record the process through videotape. I try to give the perspective that I am watching the method as it develops. It is better when you learn the process by actually watching it unfold. I add how to contact me and let me know how you are doing. I

enjoy receiving any information from other people, that may later be put in my museum collection. If anyone knows of any other snowshoe makers, please let me know.

I think that everyone should try snowshoeing to experience the amazing feeling. When using traditional snowshoes, people get a glimpse of

the past and gain a greater appreciation of this art form. I believe that I am an ambassador for the world of traditional snowshoes. Keeping this art form alive is something I enjoy doing. I accomplish this through sharing my knowledge through demonstrating, teaching, showing, and talking to people about snowshoes, year around. I make a lot of connections by drawing groups of people to listen and talk. I get to hear all kinds of stories and things people use to do. That is great! We are losing so much because the world is changing and it is hard to collect the information. Mainly old time snowshoe makers had the knowledge and much of it has been lost. The internet is convenient and you can learn a lot, but there is still not a lot of information. There need not be snow on the ground for me to give demonstrations on how to make snowshoes! There is always something to learn about making traditional snowshoes. We are still learning!

Benjamin Latvis

Crown of Maine productions, Inc

Alan & Brenda Jepson

Louise Latvis

Louise Latvis Snowshoes

Hudson and Jordan Labbe

Jordan Theriault

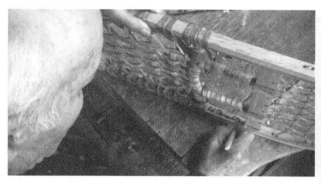

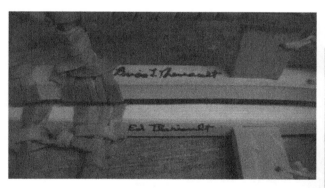

Lionel Lavoie   Joseph W. Davis

Best Wishes, Joseph W. Davis

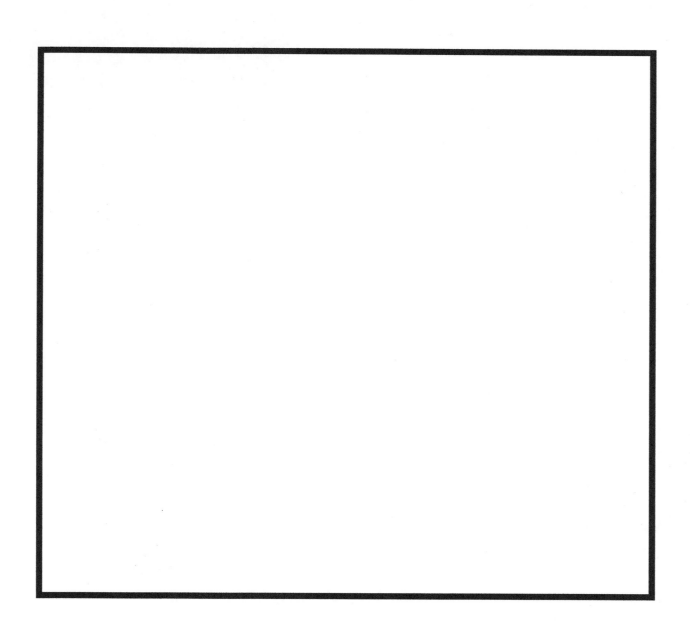

Notes:

CPSIA information can be obtained at www.ICGtesting.com
Printed in the USA
BVOW10s1303231214

380330BV00001BB/1/P

9 780991 006991